SO-AAZ-460

Mojac's Megan

Jack Judge

July 15, 2004
at Don + Connie's
in Lincoln City

Mollie-O Judge

Mojac's Megan

The Legacy of a Dog, Her Masters and Memories She Left Behind

Jack Judge

Illustrations by Mollie-O Judge

BookPartners
Wilsonville, Oregon

Copyright © 2000 by Jack Judge
All rights reserved
Printed in U.S.A.
ISBN 1-58151-025-X

Publisher's Cataloging-in-Publication Data
Judge, Jack, 1928-
   Mojac's Megan: the legacy of a dog, her masters and
memories she left behind / Jack Judge.
   p. cm.
   ISBN 1-58151-025-X (paperback)
   I. Title.
PS3554.05 1999   98-74714
813'.55—dc21   Cataloging by D. Chvatal

Cover design by Richard Ferguson
Text design by Sheryl Mehary

This book may not be reproduced in whole or in part, by
electronic or any other means which exist or may yet be
developed, without permission of:

BookPartners, Inc.
P. O. Box 922
Wilsonville, Oregon 97071

Dear reader (possibly plural) this is a true story of Mojac Farm ... which was; Mojac animals ... who were; and Mojac people ... who are.

Mollie-O and I dedicate this book to Mojac's animals, especially our beloved MEGAN, whose exuberant love of life has, we hope, been conveyed in these pages.
P. S. Some anecdotes may have been st-r-e-tch-ed. Nobody's perfect!

⇥⟫ ⟪⇤

God bless all who wade through this treatise. We are delighted to welcome one and all to the hallowed halls of: CLAMS (Canine lovers are more secure).

Contents

Megan

Prologue

It rains in Oregon! A typical winter that year — incessant rain and blow — got carried away. Black ice. Snow. Freezing rain, more rain — heavy rain — and, enough muck, mud and flood to cause Old Noah, if he'd been around, to enlarge and reinforce the Ark! Such excess awoke her. Normally Oregon's princess river, the Willamette, (which rhymes with dammit), flows serenely — gentle in her actions — through western valleys, past farms, small towns and cities, to Portland, thence on to the sea.

Usually winter, bestowing a soft kiss, reminds royalty of the impending but slight increase in girth to her girlish figure. That year a rude kick substituted for the kiss. Almost immediately, winter forced the princess to carry five times her regular weight! Such unforgivable rudeness — enraged her!

Picture a lonely ship sailing upon a heaving, endlessly gray sea. Unable to plot position from an invisible sun, incapable of satellite communication, the vessel's direction becomes wandering, aimless, lost.

The princess — laboring under that hugely abnormal load, increasing daily from ceaseless downpour — desperate for sunlight needed for navigation, totally lost her senses. In panic — blind — she reached far over her banks trying to feel her way to the sea. In the process, flowing north, she left one holy mess along her widening course.

A compassionate lady, she usually dines on slices of riverbank, grass, water lilies and — spring flowers. However, the undermining of soil, streaming away precious silt, plus carving new inlets, coves and bays, made her peckish for more. She wasn't particular as to choice from the menu. Now rampaging ruthlessly — the Willamette turned omnivorous — swallowing animals, people, houses, cars, boats, docks and trees, plus a cornucopia of bric-a-brac! Imagine what that kind of gorging does to the digestion.

By the time she reached Portland — bulging brimful, dangerous to citizens, mean, ready to crest — she threatened to turn the City of Roses into a muddy, bug-infested swamp! Praying for divine intervention, the city, frantically trying to avoid disaster, had been endlessly sandbagging herself silly.

Whew! Laughing dark clouds chose that exact moment to turn the faucet off. A glimpse of sun. Calming herself — settling for a few unladylike burps in passing — Princess Willamette joined hands with big sister, the mighty Columbia. Then — together — they continued to frolic their way to the Pacific Ocean.

Damage to Oregon? Millions of dollars. She'd been a flaming laugh a minute! Ah, yes. A typical winter in Webfoot Land? You-all come!

After that destructive, killing-mean winter mustn't rebirth follow? C'mon, how about one teensy-tiny slit in those clouds. Just enough to allow sunlight to warm damp land. Maybe it could allow color, and nudge budding and sprouting. Do we ask for too much here?

Regardless of climatic conditions — earth spins and circles. Seasons wax, wane and, in between, articulate. Nature obeys. Hallelujah!

On a smaller scale during the time of the rain's decrease, two animals performed an age-old rite.

Their coupling, intense, remained brief. Above — a full

rainbow spectrum painted diminishing storm clouds. Skye —
revered royal female, in the interim while colors reluctantly faded
— rested. The male, his ancestry true, tracing to Scot nobility, stood
guard. Mating would take place again; there would now not be the
need. Deep within her, egg and seed had joined, the pulse of life
had already begun. That rainbow an omen:—their issue would truly
spring remarkable.

MOJAC FARM

1

Meg and Her Hidey-Hole

When alla yo mite adds flight to fright it totals ... outa sight!

Mojac

"Hurry! Old Blue's in trouble. She needs help."

Breathless, having run from the cow barn from whence Megan had been dispatched to fetch me, I took in the Maternity Row scene and said,

"Sorry, love, you know my hands are too big. Besides, a lady in delicate condition is entitled to help from you, the Mojac pro. Push her over to me and I'll pop a shot of penicillin in her backside."

"I've already tried to help," said Mollie-O. "I suspect we have a breech situation. Poor Blue has been in labor a long time and she's growing weak. Do something!"

Well — ever up during an emergency — I trotted to the house, grabbed the phone and SOS'd the vet. Upon his arrival, a quick check determined that Old Blue, one of our smaller, registered

Suffolk ewes was attempting to deliver a very large lamb. The Doc soon discovered one of the babe's front legs was folded under him impeding birth even more. In a trice he pushed the lamb back, straightened the leg, slipped a loop of cord over the tyke's freed legs and encouraged Blue to push while he pulled. A large groan and a strangled baa from the ewe. Well looky there, our old darlin', labeled ancient for a sheep, has delivered not one but two luvverly new Mojac lambs. Not bad for a nine year old broad!

I draw reference to the above because my brave part in that venture drew nothing but scornful looks from my Mollie-O. I have to confess, Doc's hands were TWICE as big as mine. Hey, I was a city boy. Coping with nature there, in the city dictionary, muggings, mayhem and murder, always came before maternity!

I expect you're wondering how we got into the lamb birthing business in the first place. In order to provide understanding I'm going to carry you back about seven years — although it seems like a whole bundle of years more — to the beginning.

⇒》   《⇐

June can be tricky, weatherwise, in the Silverton Hills of Oregon. Hay ripens quickly. Farmers must reap while grass is still tender. Rain is not kind to a mowed and drying crop. (But before you leaf ahead to unearth some further joys one often experiences hobnobbing with sheep, I'd best lay a tad bit of biographical background on you to explain the title Mojac. The MO relates to the principal female person on the farm known as Mollie-O. The JAC refers to the author, Jack [me]. Thus, Mo, plus jac, reads Mojac, two reasonably intelligent people knowing zilch about raising sheep who had—literally—bought the "farm.") If, weather permitting, it turns out to be your year on an Oregon farm in the Willamette valley, needed winter feed will be cut, dried, raked, baled — then barned — before Mother Nature buckets down again. This June looked like a lucky month for Mojac. I was mowing hay in the south pasture when my wife, Mollie-O, yodeled me over to the gate. Nestled in her hands lay a small ball of black and white fluff. Two, huge, brown, expressive eyes smiled into mine and a petite body wriggled ecstatically in her firm grasp. Love bloomed warm at first sight. We promptly named this tiny tag of a purebred Border collie Megan, soon shortened to Meg unless our little miss was in disgrace whereupon many names — mostly polite — would surface. Born April 12, 1978, and a lifelong resident with Mojac eight weeks later, she bossed us around for sixteen wonderful years. Her name means "A pearl of great value." Not since the first caveman dubbed his pet tyrannosaurus, Rex, has a name proved more prophetic!

→» «←

Of course, we already had a big dog named, Peppy, but he was Mojac Farm's brave watchdog — guardian of the farm while we were absent. Peppy, a Doberman-German Shepherd cross, bulked large. He also portrayed one menacingly tough customer to mess with. Housed safely within his pen, Peppy, Mojac's thespian, hammed into an acting frenzy whenever anyone dared to try invading our (actually his) domain. His wild, blood-curdling performance was enough to color one's liver pale!

Pep's enclosure formed a secure and sturdy corral of steel posts supporting woven wire on the east, north and south, with the garage wall framing the west. His doghouse, facing west, was situated four feet away from the south fence and eight feet from the garage wall.

Whenever strangers crackled over driveway gravel, the curtain rose and Peppy's program commenced: Barking, growling and snarling, he would race around his house. Reaching the garage, then leaping, his forepaws would club the wall ... BAM! Round he would race again thumping the living sawdust from the wood on every circuit, howling at the top of his lungs. Galloping feet, scattered yard rock, snarl ... POW! Again: thundering feet, scatter-shot, yowl ... CRASH! Ferocity in those charges would have petrified Dracula! Many a hardy soul, half out of car or truck, would decide discretion the better part of valor. Crabbing back in their seats they would halloo the house until either Mollie-O or I rescued them.

In desperation, I boarded off the front corner of the doghouse to the fence, in effect, stopping his wild circling and frustrating

Peppy no end, but satisfying me. The flaming garage had already
been nearly shifted off its foundation!

⇒≫   ≪⇐

City folk enjoy visiting the Silverton Hills; many of them
head on for Silver Creek Falls, four miles away. The state park —
one of the largest in the country — consisting of countless waterfalls, hiking, horseback and biking trails, always remains popular.
Most Hill visitors are considerate, but sometimes characters bent on
mischief show up. One day a noisy beater full of possible problems
coughed into our driveway. We were working in the yard which,
considering that both activities inflict pain, was akin to root canal
for me. Resigned, I was cutting grass in back while Mollie-O
weeded the front. Peppy, buzz-sawing contentedly, lay hidden by
the front gate catching siesta zee's in the balmy summer sunshine.
These outsiders, ostensibly highway-confused, required park directions. Spying my wife by herself and feigning puzzlement at her
counsel, one of them oozed out of the front passenger seat, ambled
lazily over and planted his mitts on the gate latch preparing to enter
— uninvited. Not a good idea! Peppy, out of sight up to this time
— woke — stood when the clown started to barge in, laid forepaws
over the gate's top bar, grinned and WOOFED a halitosis, "Hi" in
that lad's face! Bozo stumbled, almost fell, then ran back to his rust
bucket. Barreling, spitting gravel, they hauled tail, desperate to get
away from second hand garlic! Yep, greetings can perhaps be a mite
too effusive. Mollie and I never worried when Peppy was around.
In truth, although only Mojac knew it, Peppy was really a big,
lovable, grinning old softy; however, he wasn't our stock dog. We
ran sheep and cattle in those days. There was a need for Megan.
Whenever she wasn't hanging on to Peppy's tail pestering him, her
natural Border Collie instincts soon began to show. So, Meg
proceeded to practice her herding skills on the barn cats who,
preoccupied with clawing about the farm as felines are wont to do,
arched backs, spat and weren't slightly thrilled with the game;
nonetheless, it was a start and Meg had a ball.

For all you wistful, city-folk readers who dream of serene
country living, one four letter word captures the essence of life on

the farm. That word is work! From sunrise to sundown there is always a chore to be done. Busy also means engrossed, which might explain why two days after Meg's arrival, we lost her. Our soft little fur ball, looming no bigger than a gentle sneeze, was, of course, not yet housebroken. Having work scheduled down in the barn that day, Mollie-O and I took Megan along with us. Once our hay was housed, it was time to shear the sheep. Then, wool required sacking, the barn called for cleaning — a most uplifting chore — woolies needed dipping and their feet clipped (more info on this later), our manure spreader needed greasing, and the cutter blades had to be removed from the old tractor. Next, dismantle the barn jugs — individual wooden pens that had housed mother ewes and their newborns to ensure proper bonding. Bummer lambs we did not need. These jugs, also called one butt pens, made those oh so necessary inoculations, along with tail docking, easier, and ensured that each baby lamb would be returned to the right Mom. Are you still with me? Creep dismantling follows: A creep is a special pen with a small door cut just big enough to permit a lamb to pass through. Soon the weaning process begins and Mom's little ones will start munching on grain, alfalfa and hay. A separate station is needed for the small fry, otherwise the big, hungry Mommas, always eager for tasty grain, will 'hog' all the feed and the lambs will get aced out.

Finally — and remember, I've described only the barn chores thus far—we were ready for the pièce de résistance, pitchforking aromatic manure into Chumley, the spreader, to be tractored out for dispersal over the pastures. Here was a delectably charming job as it was not unusual for chunks of phewey-phewey to come flying off the old spreader and smack the tractor driver (me) on the noggin!

You can imagine that, with all the fun things we had to do, it would not be hard to lose track of a smidgen of a dog. Nooks and crannies abound in all old barns. Close-doored feed rooms, hay bales, grain sacks and pen partitions to hide behind. Describe a need for storage and a barn will provide; ask any farmer! On this overfull day, after an interminable time, we straightened aching backs and thought about casting bleary eyes to where Meg had been lazing. No Meg!

Perplexed, we began to search in earnest. Have you ever turned a jam-packed barn inside out? Megan was nowhere to be found. Certainly it was too soon for her to know her name, calling would accomplish nada. "Okay, relax, not to worry," I said to Mollie-O. "If our Megan is not inside, perhaps while exploring our mighty mite wriggled out into the paddock."

We scoured every foot. No Meg! Maybe she got as far as the pasture? There were sheep in all the pastures! *It would not take much to stomp a critter only a tad larger than a mosquito bite.* After searching every foot of fourteen and a half acres, including the pond, there was still no trace of her. While I began the search all over again in the barn, Mollie-O kicked the old Dodge into gear and drove along the highway. It was growing dark and the road handled *beaucoup* traffic. Punkin was Lilliput small. Anxiety knocked.

Mollie-O

FARM
BUILDINGS

Mojac's barn had two separate rooms located over on the sheep birthing side. One contained a water faucet, shelves, kettle, hot plate, two chairs and a portable electric heater. We used this room while waiting — usually late at night — for an expected lamb to arrive. Often more than one ewe would be blessed and Mojac, most willingly, performed roll call for them.

The other room served for storing grain. Garbage cans with lids housed our winter's supply of oats, lamb creep feed, and COB, a combination mixed in molasses, of corn, oats and barley, which

fueled our growing lambs. (I confess here that Mojac spoiled the
heck out of their stock — for which we take full responsibility!)
Also in residence were twenty, two-gallon water pails from the
sheep jugs and an ancient set of scales used for measuring feed
portions. On every spare shelf and in every free corner, I'd also
crammed numerous bits of wire, staples, bric-a-brac and tools
needing protection from damp weather or, snow! Naturally,
whenever I needed *the* tool in a big hurry I never could find it!

A one-foot-square hole had been cut in the door of this room,
some twenty inches from the bottom, to allow the barn cats access
for their everlasting hunt for the resident mouse population. We
called it our "kitty patrol" door. During my first pass through the
barn, I had taken a perfunctory glance inside the store-room, for —
with the exception of that egress hole — it was always solidly
closed. Now, with nothing to lose, I decided to take a more thorough
look. That room was not wired for lights so, in the deepening dusk,
I propped the door wide open and peered into the gloom. *Hello
there!* In among all that paraphernalia, I spied two, huge — orphan-
scared eyes — peeking at me from behind the feed scales.

Despite all the turmoil, Megan hadn't made a sound. How she
had hoisted her tiny body up and through that gnomish hole beat the
tar out of us, but there she was, safe and secure in her newly discovered hidey-hole.

THE
HIDEY-
HOLE

-»> «<-

You are thinking our decision to go rural passes under-standing. Whatever possessed a city dude to buy a sheep farm in the first place? In a poor attempt to clarify, I have to sweep a few cobwebs off my mental archives and peruse a few of the pages of memory. You will be forgiven if discovered catching a short snooze here.

Still attending? Here we go back to 1957. An expatriate Canadian, born in Toronto, I was — after serving four years in the United States Air Force — residing in Yucaipa, California, having recently returned from South America, specifically the Peruvian jungle, where I'd gone to capture wild birds and animals: monkeys, jaguars, parrots, snakes, etc. to add to our bird farm from which I earned a living. Our Peruvian escape came to pass in hopes of increasing public sales of exotic animals and take a starving wallet off an overlong diet.

I'm not going to bend your ears talking at length about that menagerie as I've already put a lot of it in another book; hopefully, it will soon be published.

Suffice to say, the bird/animal farm went belly up. Still possessing a constant desire to eat after having raised a calf, some chickens, rabbits, turkeys and pigs, I had braved the real world looking for work.

Mollie-O and I met because I was working as an assistant parts manager in a Chevrolet agency in Redlands, California. Before you start laying "Good show, well done and pip pip's" on me, the department was comprised of but two troops. You can guess the other guy's title!

Have you ever heard the oldie, "If you don't think the dead come back to life, be here at 5 P. M.!"

Many businesses, supplying goods, pass slow afternoons until — precisely at closing — the aforementioned dead, crowd in at the last minute crying, "Guys, it's really an emergency, I gotta have it!"

Mollie-O, one of the dead, cruised in at 4:59:58! The agency salesmen, aware I was single, kept their eyes open looking for likely prospects for me. The married always do that, staunch believers in the old adage, "A man is incomplete until he's married — then he is finished!" Tell the truth, I kept an eye peeled, too.

Perusing a parts catalog for a phone customer I looked up and beheld this cute little trick in a ponytail hairdo. A salesman pal had intercepted her as she came breezing in through the showroom door and steered her directly to me. The parts manager was older, uglier and … married!

Seemed like this little doll had side view mirror trouble on her 1956 Chevrolet convertible (Wouldn't it be grand to have that little four wheel beauty today?) as the glass portion had fallen out. We walked outside to view the damage whereupon I informed her the mirror didn't come separately. The whole shebang would have to be replaced.

"Why is it not possible to apportion another piece of glass and simply glue it in place of that which has fallen out?" inquired the little cutie.

I knew right away she was going to be trouble!

By that time I'd learned she was a native Californian, born in Highland Park, and taught school in Redlands, which of course explained why she talked funny. No flies on me!

I further informed the little doll that General Motors had this thing about making money and they could make ever so much more of it by selling the whole mirror rather than a simple, itty-bitty, piece of glass. I convinced her to buy the whole unit. *After awhile, I also convinced her to marry me.* Wouldn't you know, like that flaming piece of mirror glass, she's continued giving me trouble for forty-two years. Not bad, huh?

Time passes: Mollie-O and I had decided to tie the knot. Three of her sixth grade students came to visit the Chevrolet agency in order to pass judgment on me, and to extend an invitation to the surprise shower they were going to hold for her in her classroom.

Those kids were absolutely priceless. I was told when to come, where I would be hidden, and how quiet I had better be until called forth to participate in the festivities. Naturally, they gave the date along with specific directions to her room. They'd planned every detail. Nothing was left to chance. Who could help loving kids like that? Here's a news flash: *Kids of today are every bit as delightful. Let no one ever tell you different!*

Whenever she talked of her students, it was obvious Mollie loved them. Soon, I was numbered among those they further bewitched. Could I have received a call? We decided I'd stay working for the agency and save for one more year. I then set off for college in pursuit of a teaching credential for myself. Thus, one year after my graduation, when Mollie-O and I moved — in 1963 — from the crowds in Southern California to the slower — at that time — pace of Oregon, we both landed teaching jobs in Salem, Oregon. And stayed with them for a period of twenty-three years. Elementary school grades for me: first, teaching in an inner city school for a period of thirteen years; later, 4-5 splits (fourth and fifth graders in the same classroom) in a rural setting for ten and one half years. In order to protect the innocent, the names of those long suffering schools shall not be listed.

Mollie became a district resource teacher, helping beginners to climb over the many hurdles novices face in the classroom. Some years later, she became an Art Resource Teacher instructing and visiting all city and rural schools in Salem.

≫≫   ≪≪

When am I going to get around to answering your question, why did the city guy buy a farm in the first place? Try these reasons:

Teaching is hard work — a truth that too few people understand or accept.

Burnout had begun to sear around my edges.

Bureaucratic nonsense intruded deeper into the instructional day.

Additional unnecessary paperwork stole even more of the instructor's time.

The curriculum — rapidly overloading with extraneous piffle — began to swell like a pregnant elephant.

I felt a need for change. In 1977, after fourteen years instructing in Salem, we bought the farm hoping that by spending more time with nature, we would ease the stress of teaching. Read on to see if we were successful.

-》》 《《-

Here in the Silverton Hills, community events rank high on our scale of fun. One such affair is the Silverton Hills Strawberry Festival in June. The farmer's meeting hall is pressed into service and most of the locals are shanghaied onto work crews engaged in building strawberry shortcakes fit to feed the masses. Load on those berries and heavy on the ice-cream! Cooks from the Silver Crest elementary school rise early to bake biscuits. Trucks head out, breasting the four winds, with loaders eager to collect just picked fruit to back up their boast that the berries at the festival couldn't be any fresher unless you picked them yourself. Freshly scrubbed, tabled and chaired — in readiness for those folks with huge appetites — the Community Hall virtually shouts "welcome." Berry dunkers form assembly lines, talking, laughing and teasing as they lightly wash the lip-smacking red jewels. Sweating dishwashers scurry to and fro, while parking attendants direct cars and buses to available spaces.

Year after year, crowds of berry lovers repeat the trek. Busloads from Eugene, Portland, Bend, the Sister's area, even the seacoast, swarm through the doors. Nobody walks away hungry after one of our generous, mouthwatering and dad-blamed good shortcakes!

Local artists display and sell their wares for reasonable prices inside the Hall. Their work is good. I ought to know — two of Mollie-O's sketches graced pages inside the Hill Cookbook, a jewel plumb loaded with recipes garnered from generations of Hill people, all guaranteed to put smiles on eager faces of, nary a bite since breakfast, starving souls.

I loaded trucks during my first year at the festival; the next one, they stuck me with berry washing. With luck, over many years, one would probably end by doing it all. Funny thing though, never once were my culinary skills solicited!

Proceeds collected are used for many worthwhile projects. The Silverton Hills Berry Festival was and still is a source of well-deserved community pride. Mollie-O and I look back with nostalgia, and more than a little satisfaction, to our days of work and fun at those festivals.

-»>   «-

Thirty years ago — before the overwhelming choke and stink of grass seed, field burning — growing of strawberries was a major industry in Oregon's economy. Our Willamette Valley and also Silverton Hills housed farm after farm. Schools paroled the students in early June. It was never because the teachers were tired (although Lord knows that was true). No, the youngsters were needed for the berry harvest. Readily available labor was a must, because the strawberries demanded to be picked when nature hollered, *"Now!"* Kids from six to sixty fanned throughout the fields picking, mouth stuffing, the luscious red fruit. I think it was one of Oregon's greatest times. It gave the kids a sense of responsibility and they earned pocket money. Many of those little delights, paying for their own school clothing, took better care of it. They dressed neatly and with pride for class. They felt good about themselves, family and classmates. Their very own bank accounts were a further source of pride.

I really have to snicker today at those who complain that schools do not teach the kids the value of money, not to mention banking practices. What ever happened to good old family responsibility? The parents whose children graced my classroom certainly believed in it. Yes, it was a rich time for Oregon. Far less, "Why don't you do it for me?" Far more, "I can do it for myself!" Bus loads of pickers discharging in the late afternoon; strawberry mouthed kids in need of baths; tired, grimy, hungry, sunburned and … *satisfied.*

Oh, of course it wasn't perfect. Nothing ever is. And you bet there were problems with young kids picking strawberries, raspberries, boysenberries, blueberries, and even much of the row crops. Some of the little sneezers lacked incentive, they wanted looking after, and sometimes needed firing. Ha! Take a good gander at many adult workers today. Strawberry fights, eating more than they picked, not picking clean, scraped knees and arms, and taking too long to gather the crop were just part of the cost of doing business in those days. The flip side was that children were involved in responsible ways and tasted their futures in the World of Work. Kids also learned how to behave in society away from school along with hands-on experience in money management.

Nothing lasts. The 'Courts' got into the act. Child labor abuse. Exploitation. Sweat shops. All kids under age fourteen — out! Uncle Sam will protect your children. He also, in rapid haste to toss the baby out with the bath water, denied them.

I, too, have read about Samuel Gompers and those, before unions, labor abuses. Horribly revolting! In fact, any person who says that white or blue collar workers do not need unions, is either no student of history, a liar, or a member of management. All sweat shops are disgraceful and they should never be allowed again. However, youngsters picking crops is in no way related to juvenile labor abuse. Federal and state judiciaries need to distinguish between protecting, controlling and *smothering*.

⇒≫   ≪⇐

Mollie-O and I were not born to farming and neither of us knew that agriculture is at all times, dicey. Diseases smite the stock, weather smites the crop. Floods and droughts drive profits down, costs only know how to go up. There was much we had to learn and soon we wondered, "will the bank extend our loan?"

Remember, Mollie-O and I both taught school. Count thirty-six years for her and twenty-four for me. Teachers' salaries have never been overly generous, which was another reason why we opted for the farm. We figured sheep would supplement our income, our bodies and brains would thrive outdoors, and farm work just had to be a cinch. Shucks, it looked like fun! Ho-hah! Were these citified outsiders ever wrong. That which looked easy nearly killed us, and not a single quarter's profit ever found its way into our empty pockets. The market for spring lamb started low and stayed mired that way for the ten years we fought and lost the fight. Meanwhile, our faithful woolies happily munched grain and alfalfa at our expense.

A choice payoff was the outdoors! Summer, winter and spring layoffs were now reserved for Mojac's major farm chores. I've used the term "layoff" because, teachers *do not* get paid for vacations and as far as I know, they never have. Classroom staff, versus classified and management personnel, are paid on contract for days worked only. Paid holidays do include: Thanksgiving Day and the Friday after, Veterans and Christmas days, New Year's, Memorial and Labor days; lately, Martin Luther King Day was added. State employees receive pay for all the above; depending on their length of service, they further benefit by receiving up to thirty days or more in paid vacations. Military services and Federal Workers are likewise granted commensurate pay as are most large corporations! I know a gentleman who was employed by a large telephone company for thirty-four years. When he retired, the firm had been paying him five weeks vacation yearly, taken in incre-ments of a few days at a time or, altogether — his choice!

Mollie-O instructed for thirty-six years. Monetary vacation bonus? Zilch! Surprised? Don't be. Teachers summer "paid luxury days" are pure cat fat!

Recently, politicians attacked our retirement benefits regard-less of their being negotiated in good faith by educators in lieu of pay raises. Thank God the courts overruled them! Regrettably, the politician's promise is — like a snowflake resting soft upon the tongue — ever impermanent.

→≫   ≪←

If you didn't break an axle on that detour, I could sure use your help. I need to fasten Chauncey, the damn cutter blades, onto Alfred, the tractor!

Preparing the ancient Farmall for mowing was one of my first rude awakenings to the realities of farming. Even after two days of threading locknuts on backward, enough grease and oil to service a fleet, four barked knuckles and one slipped disk, it still seemed I was shy one master's degree in mechanical engineering needed to get that contrary contraption going; yep, I would sooner prepare for mowing than eat! Cutter blades worked on the same theory as a sewing machine needle except they operated back and forth. When the linkage engaged the blades, danger lurked close by if the operator, careless with feet placement, stood too close to the moving slicers; that could result in prompt removal of the mower's foot! When I finally had the cutters mounted to the tractor, with some satisfaction I climbed aboard, hands on the throttle and wheel, foot on the brake, ready to mow. Now what? Engage blades. *Slowly, dimwit!* Because the cutters operate from the mower's right side, I cut counterclockwise around the field for my initial row. *Watch out for the pasture fence!* The mower blades don't take kindly to chewing on wire. I reversed direction when I started the second row and continued clockwise as I scissor-cut the balance of the tall stalks. *Maybe you should mow straight rows.* It couldn't hurt. Even after acquiring some experience, I had to bend my definition of "straight." Stuffings to all critics! Big deal if the pasture looks like a crewcut on a tarantula. This city dude is fervently praying he and the tractor will both end up at the same place and time — one of us alive!

Well, shucky darn, here we sit idling at the gate all rows bladed clean. This old tractor and I have become one. On to field number two. Whoop-de-do, a feller could get to enjoy haying. I wonder if raking is any fun? Megan, do you suppose there's a chance Mollie-O will go deeper into hock for a baler?

In truth, once Megan and I figured out that "consarned" contraption of a cutter system and learned how to change broken blades; sharpen the old ones; oil everything when needed (which was a never ending job); and carefully control my side hill cuts to avoid tilting, tipping, and ending up with the tractor sitting on top of my dented cranium, haying was — although dusty, hot, and sneezy work — really kind of fun.

On to raking, baling and loading; then stacking the bales in Mojac Farm's granddaddy barn, a truly ancient structure bursting with charming character. With my fanny parked inside, cozy-comfy on a hay bale during an Oregon gully washer, I could look outside and imagine the joyful abandon of Gene Kelly and his dancing feet in *Singing in the Rain*. It doesn't get any better than that! Yep, I really loved that grizzled old leaner of a barn. Considering the eons of hilarious work time that Mollie-O, Meg and I passed in there, it is probably only fair and just that I look back to ol' Granddaddy with reverence.

Compared to cutting, raking was a piece of cake. The tractor connection was as easy as hooking a trailer on to the back of a pickup, without hauling all the weight. Our hay rake was an antique like everything else, but turned our crop with ease unless I got hung up on a rock, or wrapped the whole shebang around a tree. I turned the cut rows twice to be sure they were dry. Wet hay rots. Wet hay in the barn is a recipe for spontaneous combustion. Big swoosh! No more hay. No more barn! There's an old proverb that says, "He who cares to stack it damp, barn becomes a one-time lamp."

I couldn't sway Mollie-O into buying a baler. I wouldn't take this too far, but sometimes you gotta listen to your wife. Uh-huh. As it turned out, for our small parcel, she was correct. The cost would have far exceeded the benefit. We elected to hire the work done.

Balers use either plastic twine, cord or wire for tying. When the machine was running, the process was labor saving, easy and quick. The bad news: they constantly jammed, requiring a lotta-ya-gotta repair time and much bad language!

As an extra safety precaution, we left the bales in the fields as long as the weather permitted, and we also turned them twice. No way was a hay fire going to destroy our old love of a barn!

Hay bales are not terribly heavy, unlike those cussed three-wire alfalfa beasties! Loading them onto the tractor-trailer was fairly easy. I would then back a full load up to the barn, stand on the trailer bed and toss the bales up through the loft door to Mollie-O. Under Megan's supervision, she dragged them to the back wall and stacked them. One job finished, on to the next.

Every time Mojac turned around, another chore stood in line. Weed the garden; paint the garage; kill the blackberry vines; repair the far pasture fence; clean the spreader; drain, scrub and refill water tubs ... or go sit on the patio swing? Naw, those workaholics ain't got time for no swing!

2

Meg and the Pond

A sheepish act turneth away wrath.

Mojac

Mojac Farm, approximately fourteen and one half acres, lay at the junction of 214 and Drake's Crossing. It was the loveliest farm you could imagine. Seven lush green pastures, fenced and cross fenced, plus four paddocks, two barns, a garage with a shop, a gas house (to keep the tractor fed), instrument shed, chicken house, a half-acre pond, self contained greenhouse (with water and heat), add a pig run, orchard, vegetable garden, and an immaculate three bed-room house. Fences and gates were freshly painted, lawns clipped, orchard and gardens pruned and weeded, and the picturesque barns were clean and fresh.

During puppyhood, Megan's greatest living joy came from hanging, teeth clamped, on poor Peppy's tail! For such a large dog, his true gentleness shone through at those moments. Wherever Peppy was to be found, a big-eyed burr would almost certainly be clinging determinedly to his tail. We soon discovered that praising

Peppy and patting his head would set his tail to wagging and launch Megan into the wild blue! It didn't phase her. Nothing ever did. An occasional yelp floated in through the window because some unkind soul had carelessly planted a tree directly in her path, but those mishaps were few and far between. Mollie-O often marveled at how lucky little Megan was. Most of her life remained injury-free and healthy.

Once in awhile though, even Peppy lost his patience and bottomed out with that living, pesky, tail clamp! On those occasions, he spun around and let loose with a deep growl. "Knock it off, kid or I will rearrange your silly face!" Miss Megan, no fool, would immediately desist and refrain from bugging our longsuffering Peppy for ... at least a full minute! Old faithful Pep never made any attempt to hurt her and she loved him dearly.

As it turned out, our main source of income had to remain our teaching careers. Fortunately, when it came time for us to report back to class, we felt our Meg had matured enough over the summer to leave her in Peppy's tender care.

At seven months, Megan discovered *The Pond*. Welcome fall rains had arrived and Mojac's half-acre oversized bathtub was brimming. Our feisty little collie was not one for baths. At best, she would stoically endure the despised dunking and then would promptly roll in the closest manure pile. Be assured, there was never a dearth of those on the farm! *Her* pond was different. When Megan discovered swimming, she reveled, delighted, caroused, sported and romped. After accidentally falling into a dive the first time, from then on our "happy otter" splash-dunked head first off the highest bank at every opportunity.

Mollie-O and I had enlarged our personal swimmin' hole the hard way, hand-wheeling rock and concrete across seven acres, one way, from the barn to the pond to build up the dam end. When we were through, we had raised the water level by two feet.

Did I mention the hard way? Consider a natural rock floor with hundreds of deep cracks. During the dry season, most of the pond's gallonage will take a hike through those cracks. An unusually dry summer and you could bet that all water would fly the coop! What to do? Have you ever spread a ten ton load of bentonite over a half acre floor ... by hand? Lord love a duck! Such a ball the two of us had! I developed so many muscles I could almost squeeze the ink from our mortgage with one hand. Bentonite is an absorptive clay that expands when exposed to liquid. Farmers also use it as a food supplement for cattle during the winter months, when not as much protein is required in their feed. With all those cracks securely clay-sealed, Megan's pond — like a duck metamorphosed into a swan — became a lovely, eight-foot-deep, permanent spa. Although the water bordered on bone-chilling at times and was downright frigid in the winter, for Megan the pool was a crazy, canine ecstasy adventure.

Even with the higher water level, the dam end of the pond still had a high bank, which Megan used for her diving board. Racing around and around the pond at full speed, she would call for our attention with a "Yahoo-you-guys-looka'-me-I'm-flying" bark, and would rocket launch herself into space. Splash!

Surfacing, our bubbling canine torpedo would slap and bite the water — barking deliriously — before swimming to the bank, climbing out, and repeating the entire process. Every time she relaunched, her joyful eyes virtually danced with excitement. Regardless of the weather, Meg was always ready for a quick, daring doggy dip. Mojac always grew tired long before she did.

THE SPLASH-DUNKER

Peppy also liked the pond, but his idea of Thrillsville was to wade in not quite up to his belly — no further. No swan dives for big Peppy, and he didn't come out smelling a whole lot sweeter either!

⇒≫   ≪⇐

Enchantment resides in old barns: Adventure, danger, birth, death, mystery, fun and intrigue; stories itching to be told. Mojac's wind, rain and snow-weathered animal bunkhouse was no exception. Megan and I spent hours in there digging for buried treasure. Betcha can't — phewey — guess what we unearthed.

A barn excites and stimulates. Megan, from when she was quite young until she was old and beaverish, never wearied of the dim, damp winter days we spent tending stock, grinding alfalfa, birthing lambs, feeding sheep, and best of all, drowsing on dry hay bales listening to rain gaily Bojangling on the metal roof.

Imagination stampedes in a barn! Whose hands and thoughts created it? Did he also build in pride or was that the barn's idea? What were the people like? Were they happy on the farm? How did they weather adversity? Did success abide on this farm? Changes: how many, how difficult, how often? What character of animal called this place home? What breeds of dogs or cats? How many disasters were overcome under this tin roof? Let your mind wander loose and enjoy the surprises you reel in.

Fear of fire is ever present in a barn. Sensibly, Mollie-O and I stopped smoking years ago, but visitors often needed to be cautioned. The barn is not the place to sneak off for a smoke. I contrived a small sandwich board sign that, coincidentally, draped perfectly across Miss Megan's back. It read: PROTECT YOUR HEALTH FROM RABID DOG: DO NOT SMOKE ANYWHERE ON THE PREMISES! In smaller print: "Culprit's first rabies shot, administered free by management, is sure to be pointed!"

To avoid the risk of spontaneous combustion, no bottles or glass of any kind would ever be laid next to the building's sides, where a searing sun could magnify and burn. Wet, damp, even slightly moist hay was not allowed to be stored inside. Air was invited to flow freely through the open doors in any and all weather.

Mojac slipped wide mouthed glass jars over the light bulbs in the barn and wired them to the rafters. Hot shards from an exploding incandescent lamp (yes, it's been known to happen) would never be allowed to fall onto straw-laden floors or onto bales of hay and alfalfa in the loft. Inevitably, it's the little overlooked safety features that do in the farmer, the barn, and the farm.

⇒⇒   ⇐⇐

Sheep are picky eaters and Mojac's were especially spoiled. Alfalfa comes in those large, expensive, three-wire bales. Our disdainful rams, lambs and ewes wouldn't eat the long alfalfa stems. Consequently, the barn housed a thumping big grinder. Early every morning, and evenings after school, I fooled those cud-chewing Suffolks into a new way to dine — mine! The grinder sat above a square hole cut in the loft floor. Nailed to the floor's underside was a four-foot long, three-foot wide, and two-foot deep chute, with a hinged door, at the worker's chest level on the floor below. While Megan chose a comfortable bale to recline on, I choked on clouds of alfalfa dust whenever I fed chunks of the woollies' din-din into the foreboding mouth of the totally unfor-giving grinder. One slip of the feeder stick — I wasn't fool enough to insert the chunks by hand — and nature's tool splintered into history. Mojac's growling mechanical inhaler gave Meg and me the galloping jimjams. Lucky ol' me, I had the pleasure of cranking the ugly beast up twice a day from late fall to early spring.

When the full chute hollered, "Hay, enough already!" Megan and I tripped downstairs, where I grabbed a five-gallon plastic feed bucket and hand scooped their special of the day from chute to pail, then dispensed the tasty contents over the barn-length feeder trough. After forty-one trips up and down the line (Megan sometimes counted twice), I filled the pail with dessert, a generous sprinkling of grain on top of the minced alfalfa. Would ewe believe they chomped down the whole gut-stuffing lot and bellyached for seconds!

All the while I ground, scooped and dispensed chow, the never patient sheep clustered outside the paddock gate, hollered and bellowed to be let in. I was never fast enough to suit them. In my brain-dead early days, I had let them wait inside the paddock. The infernal din was bad enough, but the barn door gate also swung outward. Much pushing and shoving against the woolly tide would succeed in opening the entranceway — partially — until five or six greedy mommas rushed through, bruising my tender body to the extreme and slamming the gate closed again. The rest of the irate sheep were left swearing and shouting dire threats in the yard!

After watching my futile struggles for several days, Megan had teeth-gripped my overalled leg and dragged me from the barn to the paddock gate, where she flopped on her belly and brown-eyed up at me as if to say, "Yo, dummy. Leave the sheep out here until the barn door's open." Grannies! When your dog is smarter then you are, it can surely gravel the old gizzard. Happily, ever after that eloquent message, I kept the bleating blatters outside the flaming paddock until I was ready for them. Megan got an extra dog bone that day — maybe two.

⇛   ⇚

Mojac Farm was a picture postcard, with terrific views in scope and grandeur of the Willamette Valley. Tall, farm-enclosing fir trees spoke volumes in soft whispers. Maternal sheep sounds circled pastures of spring grass as Mojac's Megan exhibited her skill and grace herding playful, balky lambs into the main barn paddock. Sunsets over the big valley were so eye-filling that only double and triple takes would make them believable.

On the Fourth of July, Mollie-O and I could enjoy Salem's entrancing fireworks, arcing, exploding and glowing across the sky, while we sat inside, snug, cool and bug free in soft chairs in front of the large picture window. Megan was content to lay at our feet, her puzzled ears perked, listening to the oohs and ahs of her masters exclaiming aloud at the beauty of the show.

Birds were everywhere: sassy jays; robins, goldfinches, bluebirds, house wrens, juncos and hummingbirds; crows, hawks; waterfowl: ducks and geese — all voicing their presence through summer's warm air. Coyotes — a lamb's nemesis, but oh, so graceful — jump-sailed over pasture fences. In the chill of winter, the trees, pond, pastures, barns, house and road were blanketed in a white and soundless splendor of snow.

Picturesque Mojac Farm was a haven of beauty. Mollie-O, Megan and I loved it well. Unfortunately, monetary concerns, constant work and lack of time eventually prevailed. Amid the heavy daily demands on mind and body, Mollie and I seldom sat to count our blessings, but through those rapidly racing years we learned to accept our licking and keep on ticking.

One thing we never got used to was the crusade by greedy counties in this state to shove the Proposition 5 property tax initiative up the noses of land owners by raising assessments excessively. Let your dwelling and property revert to a trash heap and save through reduced taxes. But if you landscape, paint, repair, and maintain your property with pride, as a bonus you pay a penalty in higher taxes. The state rewards the unwashed and the uncaring. Bathers and skivvy changers are punished. That stinks!

⇒》   《⇐

Here in Oregon, Mother Nature is a clever old broad. Every winter she serves up her full agitation, scrub behind the ears, double wash and double rinse downpours. When spring arrives, sensing the delicacy of young shoots and sprouts, she slips into her soft fabric, teardrop gentle, one wash, one rinse, kissy face rain. Mother knows her seasons, but — let me tell you, cousin — don't mess with her! Sometimes she gets a smoldering mean look in her eyes when she sees too many clear-cut forests; six-lane freeways; triple-rigged monster diesels; arson fires; muggings; killings; rip-off con games; state-sponsored lotteries; vandalism; casinos; windy, non-productive legislative sessions; violent, vulgar, raunchy TV programs and incredibly stupid commercials — and I have barely brushed the chaff off the hay wagon's floor!

When Ma Nature's eyes darken, you can bet she's fixing to pour interminably (this year has been a beaut), determined to scrub her land clean again. I admire her attitude. Turn the tap on full, Ma!

3

Meg and the Car Thief

He that pilfers another's things, resideth his head in a bell that rings.

Mojac

If I haven't yet convinced you that raising sheep entails work, tune in to the following. We call it clipping, tagging and drenching. One of our more delightful tasks, referred to in chapter one, was clipping — the paring of sheep hooves. From time to time, our fingers and toes need trimming, because the nails grow and it becomes tedious trying to pick up a fork with foot-long talons. Sheep have the same problem. Not picking up forks, of course, but left unattended, their hooves will curl to such an extent that dirt, mud, and dung will pack between the plate and pad. Ignore your sheep's feet at your peril. Serious cases spread infection resulting in foot rot, the absolute bane of all sheepmen, not to mention the woollies themselves!

A wet spring and fall required paring more often. We clipped our sheep three times during the year, and at the beginning of the breeding season we would also tag and drench. After Mollie-O and I assembled a portable chute in the cow barn, Megan would herd the stock from the paddock into a holding pen in front of the chute. Inducting one victim at a time, I push-walked them from the pen, along the portable walkway and into a sheep squeezer: a metal rack with one side hinged and a long levering handle on one end. The opposite side of the rack contained a wooden platform approximately three feet long and two feet wide, forming a bed. Once pressure was exerted on the handle, which required just enough thrust to cause a small hernia, the whole contraption tilted from vertical up to horizontal, laying the incarcerated sheep on its side, pretty as you please, with its feet sticking out ready for attention. As a safeguard, a chain, securely fastened to one end of the bed, was then hooked onto a barn rafter so as to free both hands to attend to the clipping, and also to insure that the swinging platform did not flip rudely back to the vertical, removing some of the clipper's teeth in the process! Mojac dubbed that ornery contraption, Bertram.

Don't ever ask a sheep to agree that position in life is everything. While tightly imprisoned sideways in the squeezer, no one ever tried to leave, which left us free to proceed with our party. Sheep hooves are saddle tough, and trimming the feet of a big ram was like trying to give a manicure to a polar bear! At the same time, clipping trotters was delicate enough work to rule out the comfort and protection of gloves. We frequently had to stop snipping to sharpen our shears, and by the time I finished clipping all the sheepish feet, my flaming hands looked like two hamburger patties eager for the pan. Following paring, cleaning, and bathing all those tootsies, we were ready for step two.

Snow contains nitrogen, and heavy winter amounts of the frigid glop make spring and summer grass especially rich. For the sheep, the enriched forage resulted in a good case of the *dire rears!* To prevent disease and infection, Mojac had to effect diaper changes for the flock by trimming away the manure packed wool from that delicate and oh so hard to reach area around their tail. The operation is called tagging. While the sheep were locked horizontally on the clipping rack, we did the dirty deed. Hold breath. Snip ... yuck, snip ... yuck, then shear until their backsides were definitely subject to drafts! Doesn't this sound like oodles of fun? Proceed to step three — drenching.

For this next maneuver, the poor, bemused, crew-cut and foot-clipped woolly was returned to the vertical plane and released from the squeezer, whereupon Mojac Farm's Poppa Doc (me), with consummate kindness, pried open its mouth and shoved a hooked metal nozzle fastened to a two-foot rubber tube down its throat. The tube was connected to a leakproof bag containing worming liquid. As nimbly as I could, I pumped a few shots of Dr. Clod Dogood's Elixir down a surprised throat and into what I prayed was the right cavity!

Eighty percent of what a sheep ingests comes directly off the ground. Unlike raccoons, they don't take time to wash it. The drench, or joy juice, was important for worm and parasite control. Finally the hateful, from the victim's viewpoint, closed end of our hoosegow chute opened and one by one the paroled staggered away, mumbling and gurgling to themselves. Next!

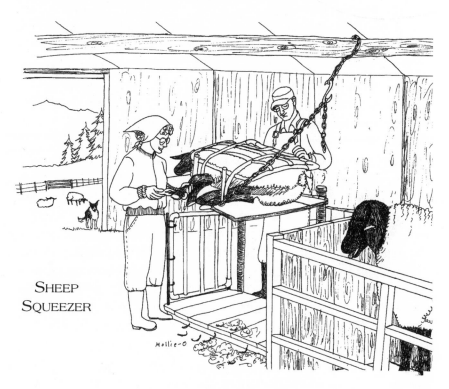

SHEEP
SQUEEZER

Mollie-O

Have you not observed by now that raising sheep keeps one busier than a flea on a new dog in town! After a hummer of a day like that, we would help one another to straighten an aching back and then take Megan for a relaxing swim.

-》》   《《-

Megan, a long way now from her puppy fleece pelt, was truly a credit to her ancestors. As beautiful a Border collie as one would ever see, and smarter than an IRS agent shooting holes in a Mojac expense claim, Megan could and also did laugh! We caught her in outright guffaws many a time. Possibly there are doubters out there among you. Please heed the following:

One summer, Mollie-O's older brother, Dave, one big, rugged troop, an ex-Marine and a good friend, Volkswagoned to Mojac Farm for a visit. On this memorable morning, Davey and I were attending to barn chores, one of which was checking on some momma ewes. There is an old adage with livestock folk: Never handy-name your farm critters, because when you lose them it hurts too much. Naturally, we'd named every flaming animal and thing on the farm! One of them was a ewe Mojac called Gutface. Being a Hampshire, she totaled out somewhere between the size of a buffalo and an elephant. In keeping with her name, this huge momma totally dedicated herself to eating. Gutface didn't have a mean bone in her body (there wasn't room), but that did not stop her from being determined. To her, food equaled ... life and life equaled ... food!

The portly old dame had taken station at the far end of the built in feed trough, which ran the whole length of our forty foot barn, for some quiet snacking. In order to examine her, I needed to corral her. Prior experience had taught me to use a portable gate and I'd provided myself with one about four feet by three feet. These, always handy, were used as sturdy partitions for the jugs. I started to hem Fatso in, but Davey advised me not to bother.

"Just "chouse" her down this way," he said, "and I'll collar her."

There is an Irish proverb, loosely translated from the Gaelic, that says, "The prudent man does not play leapfrog with a unicorn."

"Dave," I warned, "I really don't think that's one of your better ideas. Gutface is a determined old bag."

Undaunted, Davey chortled, "No problem, piece of cake, roust her big behind my way and I'll snag the old dear."

He then assumed his best Marine Corps blocking position. With extreme misgiving, Megan and I carefully edged behind Gutface and began herding her toward Mojac's "Dick Butkus". The ewe had a better idea, no Marine was a-goin' tuh git 'tween her an' grits! Dave lunged. Gutface didn't go around him; she didn't go over him. Big Momma went through him! Nothing personal mind, 'twas just the shortest distance to granola heaven. Davey ended up flat on his back in the muck and mire, arms and legs flapping in the air. I cracked up! Meg, no fool, having quietly moved safely out of harm's way, sat off in a corner canine haw-haw-hawing, with her tongue all a-flop and a silly grin on her face. Gutface, with her typical ovine nonchalance, baaed, "What's the big deal, fellers?" and placidly continued to enjoy her early lunch, completely at peace with her world. Sneaking a peek at Dave, I saw he was still feebly waving his arms and legs like a shot down fly! I broke up again. For all the hours, days, and weeks of tedious farm work, peals of hiccuping laughter — though unspendable cash in the market — still fatten an empty wallet.

DAVE AND
GUTFACE

Given our workload, you'll understand why, once in a millennium, Mollie-O and I had to escape the farm. Believe it or not, we did not enjoy a real vacation for more than ten years. The rare weekend was all we ever managed to snare, and those came only when we could con my parents into baby-sitting Mojac's critters. When we did get away, the three of us headed for ocean, gulls and sand, where Miss Megan found another wonderful playroom for pleasure. A whirling dervish, she'd spin and jump, chase and bark up gulls, slap at waves, sniff strange, fresh, excitingly new odors — then run, and run, and run!

Whenever we slipped out of the Hills for a Saturday of beach-combing, we made sure to attend Mass on Saturday night. That way, Mojac could head back to the funny farm on Sunday afternoon in time to catch the Raiders on TV. You might hate 'em, but the Silver and Black have always been my guys! When Kenny the Snake coiled to strike long, pass the flaming dip and hush your face! So, who's going to feed stock? Maybe Mollie can be coerced. If not, Megan can flaming well go and do it. Hit the bricks. Don't bother me. I'm not home!

⇒⟫　⟪⇐

After Mass one dark November evening at the coast, we found broken glass by the back door of our car in the dimly lit church parking lot. Closer scrutiny revealed that the left rear door vent window on *Megan's* Buick wagon had been shattered. Megan was standing on the wagon's deck — ruff raised — a look of sheer outrage clouding her face. The window catch now lay inside on the floor by the back seat. I had left some tools — a hammer, saw, level and some wrenches — on the floor mat in the rear of the wagon, but everything in the car seemed secure. Meg, had always been an excellent traveler. As long as Herself could be with Mojac all was well and she remained content. Left alone in the car she normally curled up against the back seat and caught some zees — usually with one wary eye open — until we returned.

Make no mistake though, that station wagon was *hers*. Bad cess to the transgressor! Understanding what had transpired was not difficult. One of Nature's throwbacks, you know the kind:

Society done him wrong — he'd been an abused child — he had been frustrated, shorted and thwarted! This clod spied a chance for some easy pickings so he smashed the window with his "gotcha sucker" carry around hammer. In the dark, what he did not see, was Megan the Alert!

Mojac's royal guardian had no doubt immediately served notice to the sleaze he had just graduated major dummy in judgment! Megan's bark was loud and serious; mix bark with outraged snarl and the sinner had better remember how to pray! A mental picture of that clown's blistered feet hightailing him away from her fury always brings a grin. I got stuck with the repair bill, if there is any justice he got stuck with a nervous breakdown and a deadly fear of all barking dogs!

THE
CAR
THIEF

I know what you're thinking. No way could that dog be as smart as this guy gurgles. Before you disparage *moi,* consider The Case of the Missing Key.

Returning home one evening about dusk I found that Mollie-O had mislaid the garage key. (We need to be clear here: if a Mojac bod goofs, it will be her, if one is always right, it'll be me.) Leave us not fret, we housed a readily available spare. Flower pots decorated all over the patio and I had stashed an extra key in one of red geraniums which graced an end of our porch swing. Smirking at Mollie-O, I strolled casually over to the stash pot and reached down for the key, which had merely been placed amid the foliage, not buried. No Key! Remaining calm as always, I parted leaves, spread stems, shook blossoms and hand dug around base and roots. No flaming key! I locked the car in the driveway — mumbled to Megan about squirrely women — and headed off to the barn to provide evening feed.

Luckily, next morning happening to be a Saturday, I could allow sleuthing time to recover the missing key. The two-storied garage had two sliding doors and one locked door entrance, as well as a firewood room with a separate egress door. Locks on both doors operated with the same key. The garage was built on a concrete slab, but the wood storage room had a dirt floor and no concrete foundation. Farm cats kept most non-paying animal guests scurrying elsewhere or — they'd become breakfast! Occasionally a small critter would ignore the feline, NO VERMIN TRES-PASSERS ALLOWED, warning signs when hunting shelter from the elements. As Peppy's pen also abutted the woodshed, few would try braving his wrath long enough to dig and nest under the shed floor. On the other hand, Peppy also vied with yo cats for the honor of the biggest snoozer of the week!

Helping in the search, Megan began to nose around the backs of both garage and storeroom. Suddenly, lowering then scooting, half her body disappeared under the shed's back wall. Snarling, hind legs digging for purchase, she reemerged dragging an object between her teeth. Aha! Behold, on display, one each pack rat's nest renting space to buttons, bits of glass, nuts and — shining bright from out the middle — a certain ... key! Now tell me that Megan is not the smartest dog in the world.

A grand, battle-scarred oldster, that garage. I spent dinkum winter hours tasking at my heavy-duty work bench in the auto quarters. Loaded with large and small sewing machine type drawers, my bench presented a plethora of treasures: glass door knobs, chains, old tools, square nails, oilcans, wrenches, and just plain bric-a-brac. When not at my bench I would be busily crafting something in the shop room out back, also part of the garage. Cozy and comfortable on nose-frosting days, it sported a radio, a woodstove, and a rocking chair (all ancient). A fellow could always escape female chatter out there. Don't misunderstand, I know ladies are desirous of imparting important matters to men, 'twas just that quiet time was required for reflection, absorption and partitioning into the old noggin — before inevitable male acquiescence!

Perusing through the garage loft uncovered evidence that Mojac Farm had once been devoted to strawberries. Before most Hill farms converted to Christmas trees, the berry had reigned — King. Nose-probing dark corners Meggie discovered antiquated fruit carriers once used by long-forgotten gatherers. We subsequently learned that, back in the thirties, itinerant berry pickers had slept and also cooked in our garage loft. Visions of workers past stirred the imagination as Mojac stood there coated in dust back in 1978.

⇛   ⇚

You've been informed that Mollie-O is a teacher and an artist. Besides keeping house and cooking, she also partnered with me to meet the needs of the sheep, including cold morning jaunts to the barn. Her labor was careful, thorough, compassionate, cheerful ... and cheap!

To reward Mollie-O, Megan and I remodeled the garage loft into an artist's studio: knotty pine for the ceiling, fluorescent lights, and new aluminum screened windows at either end for daylight, view and ventilation. I also grape-staked the end walls. Grape stakes simply represent long, rough-hewn one by two's. I laid them vertically while nailing them side by side across the whole of each end wall. In effect, the result portrayed a rustic design. You had to be there to truly appreciate. Next, I installed a lighted drawing table, painted the side walls, added a new oil stove, then tackled the stairs, which were wide but lacked a railing and for safety, required attention.

Megan and I took a stroll to the wooded side of one of Mojac's pastures. After haunching and studying for awhile, Meg finally decided on a gnarled, but straight, fourteen-foot alder that would make a suitable railing and match the garage's venerable stature. I peeled the bark, hand sanded, polished, waxed, and then, respectfully bolted the new railing to the stairway wall. Hot smash! A certain female wasn't the only artist on the old homestead. By the way, in case you missed it, the illustrations interspersed among the pages are all Mollie-O's.

⇒⇒ ⇐⇐

Ready for early winter choring? How about feed the animals, shovel unexpected snow, try to prevent the well pump from freezing its tutu, rescue a sheep lying on its back in the snow (when prolonged, it's sayonara time for the ewe) that Mojac almost missed and, courtesy of a mainly cold wet climate, layer barn floors with fresh straw once, sometimes twice a day. Could a body cry for relief? We took a break and drove into town and let the restaurant prepare lunch. On our way back up the hill — for entertainment — we fought black ice while slipping and sliding all over the highway. Mojac Farm's circular drive was the most welcome sight in the world!

Gratefully unclamping numb hands from the wheel and disembarking, we harkened to Megan and Peppy tolling the bell of trouble from their pen. My first thought was Fire! but there was no sign of smoke. Had Mojac been ripped off? Not with Peppy on guard. Finally, I decided to check the stock.

Releasing Meg from her pen I said, "C'mon girl, let's count sheep heads."

When I reached the pasture, the problem was immediately evident. Some dummy (me!) had forgotten to make sure the two rams were separated, not just by fence but also by pasture. Boss ram, the guy with all the dollies, had been left to graze in a field adjacent to one occupied by the unfavored swain. The rival, besides not being a real buddy of the lucky one anyway, missed the ladies. A woven wire fence had kept them apart, but it wasn't enough. Yelling awfully bad language, the unrequited had gulled Romeo over to the fence and belted him, wire and all! Romeo responded in kind, air-mailing a kiss right back to him:

"Here's a fat wart to beautify your ugly nose, Accordion Beak!"

"And here's a passionate smooch to decorate yours, Clyde the Clown!"

The party had then waxed. When two hornless rams run their heads together, the sound is comparable to a couple of telephone poles traveling with express train speed colliding head on in the middle of a long tunnel. Ba-a-a ... WHUMP!

The fence was still standing although the antagonists, top-hatted now, were wearing parts of it. Blood was here, blood was there, blood was every-bleeding-where! Megan and I herded the inconsolable one into the barn, cleaned and "iodined" (I hope it hurt!), soothed with extra grain, and then back-pastured him far away from the other slugger. Romeo hadn't been dented too badly, so I washed him off — totted him a stiff shot of iodine as well — then let his dollies soothe the big jerk! Yes indeed, there was never a dull moment on Mojac's tranquil, darlin' little farm.

⇒》 《⇐

Another never ending job on the farm is equipment repair. Machinery can be so devious in its insurrection, always breaking down when you can least afford it. Even though I strove long and hard, and Band-Aided lavishly during the wet days of winter, I accomplished little that the first test of spring couldn't undo. Most of our old relics needed major surgery (including lobotomies for the owners), but I continued to live in hope and die in despair.

⇒》 《⇐

Along the way, I learned the value of a trusty workbench from my old, rugged, vice-holding friend. I almost timed the passing months availing myself of its suggestions on lawn mower upkeep: belts, blades, tune-ups, lube, oil change and, a must, rust prevention. Tractor cutters: broken blade replacement, the rest sharpened, rivets hammered tight (loose blade movement would skip-cut hay). Metal gate parts: bars, hinges, swing chains straightened or replaced. The tractor power takeoff — which was my number one nemesis — serviced, oiled and greased; its gears Allen wrench tightened with extra TLC, hugs and kisses. Fat chance! For ten years out in the field, always in the midst of hurry-before-it-rains haying, when I was most in need of take-off power, that sucker always took off! I hastened to absorb further knowledge my wooden friend imparted as to the care of Mojac's odoriferous manure spreader, for that was a piece of equipment we definitely couldn't do without!

Far, far too often that ancient, beat-up, oil-soaked fount of inspiration listened patiently as I bellowed many bad words over skinned knuckles. But I couldn't blame my workbench. That slab of wood was a true friend. Listen, at times I just up and wanted to kiss the lovable old thing!

4

Meg and the Beach Bum

If ewe will be kind, lamb children all mind.

Mojac

I do not like moles or gophers. More precisely, I detest all moles and gophers. To be absolutely clear, I hate the little landscape-destroying, buck-toothed, bug-me-all-the-time rodents! With murder definitely in my heart, I fiendishly waged unremitting, take-no-prisoners war on them and all their relatives. Megan, that disloyal, ungrateful cur, chose not to support me in my endeavors. After a single, well-aimed dirt clod bounced off her beezer, she recognized a superior foe and retired from the battle. While I struggled valiantly on, she trotted off to bug Peppy, who also was no help against the enemy though not for lack of trying. His jumbo feet moved like pile drivers, but availed him zilch as he excavated enough earth to insert two Holland Tunnels!

I finally decided that victory would be up to me. I tried traps, gas, road flares, flooding, buckshot, rock and roll music, and pepper! When none of those worked, I wept, pleaded, invoked the gods, made promises I couldn't keep, spit, swore, screamed ... and lost!

Meanwhile, the miserable little twits excavated from one end of Mojac to the other, decorating our picturesque little sweet patootie farm with trenches that resembled a World War I battlefield.

Lest you also suffer and despair, there just might be a touch of sun amidst the gloom. Recently I have been using whirly-gigs on my parents' farm. I think they hinder but do not halt the contemptible, garden wrecking sods. I discovered an even more promising solution at the local Pot and Posy nursery the other day — a battery operated, torpedo shaped unit that when inserted into the ground emits a high frequency, intermittent squawk, which is supposed to send the Go-Mo's over to play in your neighbor's yard.

Did I buy one? You bet your bippy! Thirty-three bucks plus four D-size batteries. It has been beeping its little head off for two weeks now, and I haven't seen a new mound yet. May I, might I, should I, dare I ... hope?

⇒⇒   ⇐⇐

Lambing time on Mojac Farm was a truly wondrous, joyful, magical experience. That's from my perspective; I didn't ask the ewes! I think they approach their big event happily though, for, only during birthing does the ewe talk to her lamb(s) in a guttural, sing-song voice — a wonderfully sweet, maternal sound. Often she will call out before the birth, almost as though saying, "Come on Little Baa, let's get the show on the road." Normally a mother ewe will start crooning immediately after the lamb is born. Her aria soon segues into, "Well, will you look at what I've accomplished. Girls take note, cast your peepers on a really handsome baa-a-by. Now, Junior, let's get you cleaned up and on your feet for respectful admiration, besides, it's lunchtime." The other ladies crowd around ooh-ing and aah-ing something fierce. Everybody is in a party mood and just full of the happys. Every one, that is, except maybe the overdue for sleep hospital staff — they being Mollie-O, Meg and me — when the joyful event occurred at two o'clock in the morning!

Fumbling novices at raising sheep, we had an awful lot to learn, and sometimes unlearn! Professionals, excuse the term, had instructed us to run our ram and ewes together in July, thereby ensuring Mojac lambs would be forthcoming in November or December, depending on when exactly the ewe had been caught zigging instead of zagging. What they hadn't told us was the secret to flushing — a carefully designed program for feeding prospective mothers extra nutrition in grain for two weeks prior to introduction of ram. In theory, scheduled flushing would bring all ewes into season pretty much at one and the same time. Papa didn't need any such encouragement!

Once our ewes had been flushed and sparking begun, the ram would waltz around pastures with a dazed and happy look on his face for two weeks before going back to dreaming! A poor alternative without the extra grits would be one blissful looking ram from mid summer to late fall and — lambs arriving from snow to ... whoa — we don't want any mo'! Until we learned, and adopted the flushing practice, that's how Mojac lambing was. Our very first lamb arrived at midnight on Christmas Eve. Naturally, we dubbed him Nicholas. The lambing season stretched from Christmas to spring layoff that first year.

How involved is lambing? Let's follow a birth from the beginning. First of all, banish your Border collie from Maternity Row. After flunking diaper folding, Megan's help was superfluous.

A ewe indicates her impending visitation by growing restless. Constantly on the move, she will lie down, rise, circle, then lie down again. Eventually, her water ruptures and the wondrous miracle begins. Most ewes, especially old hands, are independent, preferring to handle matters on their own. However, some lambs — mostly singles — are large and may require some help. It was not unusual for a first timer to stalk over and stare at Mollie-O and me as if to say, "Don't just sit there, Dumb and Dumber, can't you see I need yo' help?" Despite what you may have heard sheep are far from stupid. It always disturbs me when animals, treated harshly and with cruel indifference, are quickly labeled dumb. Our farm woollies were sweet, gentle friends. Mollie-O and I will treasure our memories of Mojac's sheep for the rest of our lives.

A lamb's arrival signals the event of many things happening in one heck of a hurry. Mother starts her song: "Hey-ho little baby, how do you do? This is yo momma and I'm talkin' to you." Then she begins to clean the newcomer. We help by washing mucus from the lamb's mouth and nose to ensure unblocked breathing. Mom routinely severs the cord herself, but if it's her first delivery, Mojac may have to employ their scissors. Baby presented, afterbirth disposed of (mother may do this herself, if not, we will bury it), ewe and tiny lamb(s) must then be housed in one of the reinstalled jugs over on Maternity Row. There, Momma's teats are stripped free of their lanolin wax plugs, allowing her milk to flow freely. Next, a thorough exam for a nasty condition called mastitis is performed. Vet, James Herriot handled many a case. A tyro, such as myself, will simply relate that mastitis is a serious inflammation of the teat that can impede or completely block the mother's milk flow. Most ewes display only two dugs, but single lambs can survive and thrive even if only one is producing. With twins, however, a plugged teat can beget disaster. Further woe for the farmer — the cure rate for mastitis is not encouraging.

Enough already, this ewe, healthy, has presented Mojac with twins, one luvverly duo indeed! Do you wonder how we con mom into the jug? Piece of cake, even if she gave birth on the far side of the barn, separate and away from the jugs, simply lift the tykes and let mother see and smell them. Then slowly, babies in hand, head for a jug, all the while allowing the ewe a clear view of her lambs. She will follow — bellyaching every foot of the way — right into the freshly cleaned and bedded (with straw) jug. Once the new family is safely penned, it now becomes a touch critical. Both lambs must be placed on mom's faucets in order to chug-a-lug the all important colostrum. This — the first flowing of mother's milk — contains all the nutrients along with nature's antibodies needed to ward off disease and sickness from our ewe's priceless pride. You must be sure to do this carefully and correctly.

Here's how it appears from the lamb's perspective: You catch your first glimpse of daylight about the same time you're landing on your head! Right away somebody sticks a cold finger in your mouth and up your nose. Then you're snatched up and lugged away into a dinky little pen, where a warm, soft tube is shoved in your mouth. A finger strokes your throat to make you swallow.

"Hey that tastes pretty good! Maybe things are looking up!"

"Ouch! An ugly old bozo just shoved a big needle into me. That hurt!"

"He stuck that string on my stomach into a bottle full of brown liquid, too. And that flaming well smarts!"

"Hey! Get that squeezing rubber band off my tail. This is living?"

The needle injects a shot to prevent white muscle, a mean disease quite prevalent in newborn lambs. Mojac must have done something right, we never suffered through a single case during our ten years of working with sheep.

As quickly after birth as possible, it is important to dunk the remnant of the lamb's umbilical cord into iodine to protect against infection from feces, bacteria or soiled straw.

Docking — removing the tail — while sounding cruel is most necessary to prevent caked feces from packing up the little tyke's hind end, as mother's milk is quite rich. Using a rubber band performs painless — after the initial squeeze — and in due time, circulation ceasing in that area, the tail will drop off by itself. Mojac much preferred this method over cutting then searing the stump which — much like branding — laments out sorrowful! Finally, mother and babies are ready for a well earned snoozeroo. Clean straw on jug floor, fresh water and feed for ewe, tiny lambs bedded down, Mollie and I march on to the next customer. Would it be unusual to handle six or seven births in those early hours of morning before snatching a bite of breakfast and heading off for a full day of teaching? Naw. It carded out par for the flaming course! Truthfully, on some of those classroom days, I would find myself nodding off during afternoon lectures. As they were my lectures, it proved to be somewhat embarrassing especially when my little sneezers would whisper, "Shhh. Don't wake him up." I never did figure out if that was because they were taking pity on me or, they weren't that wild about my homilies! Our friends often remarked we were nuts, driving ourselves at such a killing pace, but I don't know, except for a disconcerting twitch — today I'm perfectly ... normal!

⇥≫   ≪⇤

At long last another weekend at the beach. Hallelujah! The weather checked in perfect — blue skies, sunshine, and comfortably warm. Combers rushed in and waved as we barefooted over sand. Sandpipers scurry-stepped claims, while overhead a large squadron of screaming gulls swooped, circled, climbed and dived, replaying the Battle of Britain. So I perhaps wax poetic. Gimme a break! It was that kind of — thank you — day.

Megan, now fully in her prime articulated a classic Border collie to behold: Tip of tail, chest, ruff, legs and muzzle displayed white; long, silky, black fur covered the rest of her body. She weighed about forty pounds. Ears were pointed and stood rather than flopped. Her tail plumed, excluding only when stalking and working her charges, then she lowered it close to the ground. Eyes, warm brown, were soft and intelligent. When facing down a challenger they flamed and literally voiced her opinion. Viewing our Megan, sunset over the Grand Canyon paled by comparison! Megan was gorgeous, the day was gorgeous, the beach was gorgeous ... and then along came Gorgeous!

Dave, Mollie-O, Meg and I were toe-strolling the shoreline. What else would you do at the Coast? Surely you would not waste any precious time throwing money away in a casino! Besides, Megan had already chosen the agenda. For a sheepdog inlander — she purely had a passion for sea and sand.

I firmly believe that leashes and dogs belong together, especially in heavily traveled public areas. Gorgeous, a cute little dude about Megan's size, ran free. He was a professional beach bum! He bounded up to Megan, dancing and prancing, then woofed.

"Hiya, sweet babe. Dan's the name and running is my game. I can outdo, outdance, outrace, and outjump anything on four legs, especially a slowpoke like you. I am willing to give free lessons. Dare to care to get it on — Toots?"

"In your face, Mac. Seeing is believing!" yapped Megan. Then she looked at us in silent entreaty. Mojac recognized that look: a dare is a dare. We turned her loose and aw-a-a-y they tore. My, oh, my, how I wish you had been there. Both dogs wore virtual big buck Nike Air's on their feet. Startled gulls squawked and fluttered. Sand flew. And the canine duo flew! Gorgeous — the bon vivant — was good. Mojac's Megan was better! (C'mon, you knew she would be.) Round and round, up the beach and back; kicking in the afterburners, away they raced again — oh, 'twas surely the great, grand lollapalooza of a romp.

At last Gorgeous Dan — coast pro — collapsed, totally out of gas. Speedy Megan was still full of it: chasing her tail, gull flushing, and barking happily. The final act, a coup de maître. Mincing coyly up to Dead Dog Dan, she reached out with her forepaw and gently tapped him on his back.

THE BEACH BUM

"Hey, ol' dude, time's a-wasting, let's get your played out frame up off the sand." Gorgeous didn't move. The running lad knew that had is had!

Leashed again and trotting on, Megan kept looking back but lover boy was still out for the count. He had forgotten a cardinal rule which — applying to us all — helps to make living bearable. No matter where we go or what we do someone always looms bigger, better, smarter and tougher. Of course victories, small and large, do elate. There will also be those defeats. In between and certainly often, our conceits shall be humbled. Accepting this rule as fact — while not doing much for the ego — does make life easier to endure and isn't that what life really is? Some highs, some lows and, in the main, patient endurance. Do I oversimplify? Maybe. But today's violent anger — especially that expressed at sporting events, even though some is deliberately encouraged by greedy promoters — appalls me! I can't help thinking living blossoms better when we all learn to "grin and bear it" more. If, as stated, life is a bowl of cherries desirous of being swallowed now — and whole — the prudent would be wise to pit them first. Sure that takes more time; still, there's far less chance of choking!

Returning from our walk, we observed that Gorgeous Dan had gone. I felt a touch of remorse; he had never been tried and found wanting before.

5

Meg and the Jumping Steers

A pelt in the sack is one less to hack.

Mojac

Did you catch the eleven o'clock news the other night? The local TV pundits reported the results of a lengthy study — well researched and documented — that verified the top dog in the smarts department is none other than the cerebrational Border collie. Take heed, dog lovers. Megan came out number one. Ha! I could have told them that sixteen years ago, saving them oodles of dough and boodles of time spent on their study.

⇒≫　≪⇐

Shearing was beaucoup fun for Herself and a pain in the you-know-what for Mollie-O and me. It's hard, hot, sweaty work with far too few ho-ho-ho's and way too many dad-gum-gums! Once again it was time to shoot the chutes with sheep. Needing to separate mothers from lambs we locked the fat little rascals in the

creep after their morning feed. Weather remains calm and fairly
cool until about midsummer in the Hills; consequently, lambs were
not sheared. Mom and Pop, on the other hand, were more than
ready for a Mojac Mohawk special. We employed the equipment
shed for the peeling process. It was easier to enclose and the chute
led over, with minor modifications, directly from paddock to
holding pen to shed.

⇒≫   ≪⇐

Setting up the wool sack was interesting and not complex;
however, as the climbing pole kept swiveling, I nearly destroyed
my fleece-burdened body scrambling one-handed up that swinging
swayer! That contrary contraption consisted of a tripod of round
metal poles each about twelve feet long (and consequently ten feet
tall when erected). Each of the three legs slipped into hollow
pieces of pipe welded to a circular steel band which formed a ring
at the top. A burlap bag, itself about eight feet deep, was suspended
from the ring by pulling the mouth of the bag up through the center
of the formed tripod and then stretching it over the outside of that
ring down about one foot all around. Another slightly larger band
was then slipped over the encased outside and lowered onto the
protruding pipe welds — in effect, locking the sack in place. Or so
I hoped! This unwieldy structure was then picked up and located,
teepee fashion, on the ground adjacent to the shearing shed.
Suspended between tripod legs our now open mouthed wool bag
waited eagerly to receive goodies. I was chosen to supply them.
One of the tripod's legs had a series of short — and I emphasize
short — welded metal rungs, which formed a ladder suitable for
use by a Barbary Ape! Once those legs were inserted into the
hollow welds they normally secured with bolts slipped through
holes previously drilled in pipe and leg. As this diabolical killer
belonged to the shearer — the bolts were long gone! Naturally, in
lieu, sixteen penny nails substituted. He didn't have to scale the
miserable beast! Yep, circumference of nails less than diameter of
bolt holes. Result, tripod leg did the Big Watusi every time I
ascended!

TOTE
THAT
BALE

When the sack partially filled, I had to climb that swaying dancer, drop down inside the bag and compress the wool by foot stomping in order to make room for more. Next came the fun part, how to climb back up and out of that chiropractic horror!

Our shearer was a good guy, albeit a self-made man having not much use for teachers. Who does? He would tie himself in ha-ha knots watching me trying to escape that lousy sack. Upper body strength was not one of my strong suits. I could spell muscles, that didn't mean I had any. Eventually, hooking elbows over the steel band, I would grunt clear down to my toes and hoist myself far enough up to where I could nose-dive my flabby bod free of the damn thing! Sneakily stealing a quick gulp of oxygen, I staggered over, grabbed a fleece, tied it into a bale, and skinnied back up that flaming pole! Between times, of course, I jumped into the shed, collared a ewe and dragged her over to the barber. My prospects for survival were fifty-fifty at this point. Prone on the ground after my eighth nose-dive — suffering only a mild concussion — I proceeded to take stock of the situation. For one thing: I now had first hand knowledge what fun it had been climbing the rigging to the crow's nest in those long ago sailing ships! Two, the more wool I now stuffed into the sack, the easier it became crawling in and out of that suffocating tomb! All in all I figured I was ahead of the game. Then came the rams. Mojac supported five of the huge delights ranging in size from small ponies to a woolly hippopotamus!

Beau was the farm's patriarch and a true sweetheart. He was slow, huggable, gentle. He was also the hippo! I wobbled about one gasp away from demise when we got to Beau. That ding-blasted sack bulged full. We were now reduced to using gunny sacks for all the remaining fleeces, and only Big Poppa left to shear. Normally a sheep is dumped on its backside, dragged over, then handed off to the shearer who — being already positioned for another customer — wasted no time with the clippers.

"La hora's mucho dinero," the barber would quote. "Time is money." Anyone care a rip for my time?

He returned to mind an auto mechanic I chanced upon many years ago during college days. One day my old flivver, coughing and snorting, indicated a dire need for oxygen. Huffing and puffing, we limped into an agency garage. While my wheezing one received a transfusion and a shot of reviving vitamins, the mechanic asked me how I made my living?

"I am attending college, studying to become a teacher," I answered.

"Oh, yeah, one of those." he sneered. "And I suppose after a couple of years you'll be taking one of those fancy trips to Europe on a summer vacation."

I've already mentioned that teachers don't get paid during summer layoffs, so you can imagine how his attitude made me feel. One gets used to that bilge after awhile, but it still hurts. After all, this mechanic had attended school somewhere, and certainly a teacher had at least taught him how to add. Believe me he had no trouble at all totaling his "figgers"!

This encounter took place years before I started taking headlong dives out of wool bags, my brain worked a tad quicker then. Sweetly, I replied,

"Better yet, I should graduate as an auto mechanic, in two years I'll own Europe!" Score one for our side.

Back to Big Beau and shearing. How do you persuade a sheep to sit down? I tried shouting, threats, bribery and bad language. No way! I tried standing beside a ewe, picking up her forefeet and toppling her over. We both nearly landed in the middle of next week with that method.

Pitilessly, my learned shearer friend said, "There is only one good way to sit a sheep down. Put your thumb sideways in its mouth, place your foot behind its hind foot, twist the victim's head and then hunker back. Ram or ewe will become a cooperating obliger and sit right down."

"Put my thumb in its mouth! You are out of your sheep shearing mind! The sucker will bite the bleeding thing off," I bellered!

"Nay, nay, city dude," he laughed. "There is a dandy gap between the lower incisors and the back molars. If you insert your thumb in that gap — while the sheep may gum it up — you won't lose it."

Closing my eyes, gritting my teeth and uttering a mental good-bye to my thumb, I tried it. I'll be a three phrase jabberwocky if the darlin' lad wasn't correct and it worked a treat. Shove a gloved fifth digit in their mouth, block their feet, twist their head, down they go. It sure-fired. Chalk one up for his side!

I thumbed, blocked and twisted my way through the entire flock until I came to Beau. When I tried it with him he just stood there — docile, placid, immovable

"Aw c'mon big guy. Look, my thumb is in your mouth, my foot is behind yours and I am twisting your granite head! Beau, please let me twist your head." No way, Jose. It would have been easier to turn one of the heads on Mount Rushmore! Finally, with a disgusted look tossed in my direction, our robust shearer strolled nonchalantly over and handled the hippo himself. Making myself promise not to hate him too much, I also wrote a mental note to flush the moths from my wallet and buy some weights!

BLIND MOMMA

Once the ewes were safely secured in the shearing shed, the lambs were released from the creep and turned out to pasture. Too young as yet to wean, while Mojac sheared their parents, they browsed and played with only an occasional lonesome baa for Mom.

Lambs rate wizard fun to watch grow. Catch Me If You Can and King Of The Castle were favorite games along with Jumping Up On Mother's Back; I would always stack extra hay bales in the barn for climbing; our Pucks' would amuse themselves by the hour decking and knocking one another off the tops.

Shearing complete, wool sack tied and stored, equipment cleaned and put away, it was time to turn the shorn ewes out to pasture. Paint yourself this mental picture as finally the fun begins: A flock of naked sheep who have been caught skinny dipping. For starters, they felt good. Released from their heavy, wool, winter coats, free of the confines of the shearing shed, nary a stitch on, the sun warm upon their backs, Mojac's woollies flipped! Recollecting their past happy lamb days, mothers gamboled, played and jumped straight up in the air, emulating exactly their own current crop of babies; mincing, prancing, they waltzed through the gate into the lamb pasture, singing the mommas' chorus. Young and old converged. Then, starring in the Undress Ball, produced by PANDEMONIUM, our sheep went bonkers! Such a hollering, crying, running, bawling hubbub. Mothers sporting in the buff, the little ones didn't recognize them! Lambs bleating for mom scurried here, mommas blatting for their lambs scurried there. Dust flew, birds coughed. Sure, 'twas the grandest mix-up that ever you have seen! And all through that hilarious melee du jour, Meg, her head through the fence and Mollie-O and I leaning on it, laughed ourselves silly.

By and by, families were squared away, peace and quiet reigned and serious grazing began. It was time to release the rams. They were a different sack of oats entirely. Also sveltely attired in their birthday suits, bunkies do not recognize former bunkies. What recourse awaits? Correct. Completely nondiscriminating, they commence head bashing any and all rams in sight! Occasionally, friendly noggin bonking could, and often did, terminate in one of those bonkers shuffling off to that great party pasture in the sky, which could become downright expensive for Mojac.

With Megan's help, a dandy solution to these barroom brawls surfaced. We penned the big guys all together in small, crowded, tenement style quarters — so close they could not turn around to pound the ugly stranger standing next to them. In twenty-four to thirty-six hours, on spare rations but supplied all the water they could drink, they not only looked alike — they smelled alike! The old nose had told and, released to pasture recognized friends once more, peace reigned. With maybe just an occasional friendly thump, only to keep in shape, Mojac's rams were back to dreaming about ewes!

⇒⇒   ⇐⇐

An ancient, cast-in-granite, sheepmen's law reads: *Never turn your back on a ram!* Did Jack ever gaze yonder to the east while a ram grazed over to the west? But definitely. Reminder day for me arrived abruptly, painfully, and ended muy pronto. My back turned, I was busily scrubbing a water trough in the tough guys' pasture. The trough stood in a corner, about four feet from a woven wire paddock fence.

Suddenly … *whop!*

Learning to fly in one easy lesson, I cleared the tub and crash-landed headfirst into those unforgiving wire strands. In my mindless way, I had stationed Herself outside the ram pasture gate. Naturally, Megan was busting a gut watching me peel my bent body off the flaming fence! A tad bit perturbed, I swung around and belted the perpetrator in the chops with the cleaning brush. Then I sprouted madder still because I had to chase the big lummox all over the field to make sure I hadn't broken his jaw! Life on the farm, it purely do be fun.

⇒⇒   ⇐⇐

Given Megan's druthers, I think she truly enjoyed herding cattle better than sheep. She used to scare the tar out of me as she dodged errant hooves. Not to worry, though; our artful dodger took it all in stride and — never once swallowed a flying hoof!

Raising beef for your table is rewarding if you are not dumb enough to name and make pets of them. I've already pled guilty to that foolishness! Please to make the acquaintance of Filet and Mignon. The two, Mojac looked forward to enjoying for dinner, were lovable goofs with a penchant for grain. Low fat Holsteins, the duo also medaled as high jumping Olympians. Clearing a four-foot fence was child's play for those spring loaded Nijinsky's.

Four o'clock in the A.M.! A ringing telephone. A laughing voice softly cooing, "Your steers are loose on the highway again." I won't mention what was cooed back! Up, dress, and go collar the silly galoots. Foolishly, I once roped one of those bovine gallumpers and abruptly found my body soaring seventeen yards ahead of my feet! I canceled that brilliant idea in a hurry. We daren't use Megan, a busy highway was no place to perfect her herding skills. Mollie-O found a temporary answer. She tootled down to the barn and covered the bottom of a feed bucket with grain, the equivalent of double chocolate chip cookies to our high jumpers. Mollie-O dangled the bucket under eager noses, tramped the road to the nearest Mojac gate, and Frick and Frack trotted demurely along behind like well behaved students on a field trip.

JUMPING
STEERS

A week later — for a special dessert — I installed an electric fence which promptly sparked their interest! Megan heartily approved and because the "howdy" wire was located near the top of the posts, she never got zapped. Poor Peppy, on the other hand, frequently forgot. Standing up, he'd place his forepaws on the hot wire — briefly. With a startled yelp he would come running over to me for help in catching *the son of a bee who had just stung him!*

⇒》 《⇐

Phase one in preparing Mojac's flock for summer was, of course, shearing. With our ewes now adorned in their petticoats and the rams in boxer shorts, it was off to set up for phase two.

By now you are familiar with three of the quartet: clipping, tagging and drenching. Stand-by, here comes dipping. The big sheep conglomerates — the guys with the big bucks — dip-dunked correctly. A large excavation is bulldozed out, with runways graded at each end. Concrete is poured into forms and onto the floor to create a holding tank three to four feet deep. Runways are grooved to provide traction for the animals, a bad slip could result in a broken leg. Sheep are run down one runway, totally immersed in the tank, now filled with a dipping liquid of copper sulfate and water, then herded soaking wet up the sloping far end of the tank. From there, they are walked back out to pasture. It's quick. It's easy. It's not how we did it at Mojac Farm. However, our system, a Micky Mouse jury rig, got the job done!

The farm was equipped with some permanently attached loading chutes, a skosh bit wider than a sheep, and interspersed throughout with hinged gates. Using those gates Mojac could run the flock all the way through, from one paddock into another, or partly along, up a ramp and into the racked bed of our stock carrying pickup.

The chutes gates were constructed of one solid piece of wood — kind of designed with the dentist's door theory in mind — so that sheep could not see through or over. Provided the dentist muffles a patient's moans behind a closed door, I would most likely stay and await my turn. An open door, loud moans audible, waving feet clearly visible, and I'm bugging out! It should come as no surprise that Mojac sheep felt exactly the same way.

How do those with limited funds dip? Simple. We had a steel tank made — three feet wide, six feet long and six inches (tootsie depth) deep — which we placed on a bed of gravel between two of the chute gates. Mollie-O and I filled the Little Tootsie Dipper and our garden backpack sprayer with copper sulfate and water. Donning rubber boots, I yodeled, "Yoo-hoo," to the unsuspecting flock and began another festive day.

Sheep are dipped to thwart foot rot and discourage ticks. In the grand scheme of the universe, I freely admit I do not understand the reason for ticks. Of what use is a tick other than to Mother Tick and all her tiny Ticks? I am aware of Alexander's bit about all creatures; regardless, a tick is a nasty piece of work. I mean, for pity's sake, they're blood suckers. They infect sheep with debilitating liver fluke, the whistling fantods, dire palpitations, googurglitis, the shivering skitters and possibly — political aspirations!

Megan walked the bathers into the chute. Mollie-O sent them past the first gate one at a time. Spying the open "dentist's door" and the tootsie dunker now in clear view, it sometimes became necessary to administer a gentle nudge to the hesitant wader's derriere to encourage a step forward. With my rubber boots on, I stood in the tank waiting for customers. The boots worked gallantly at keeping the copper sulfate off my feet, but offered scant protection against clumsy hoofs. On more than one occasion — most notably when waddling Gutface stomped on both feet at once — the lovingly affectionate, "You rotten old ... hippo!" reverberated round the valley educating neighbors in rare nuances of the English Language. I could hardly wait for Beau!

Once a ewe was in the bath, her feet soaked and absorbed the magic elixir while I sprayed her body from end to end and points in between, being careful to avoid the eyes. Having completed a dipping, I'd open the escape gate and one more sopping one would trot into the paddock to drip-dry in the sun. Rube Goldberg would have been proud of our nifty little setup.

Accommodate the rams next. Lambs were always last to dip. By that time, Mollie-O, Megan and I were bushed, but baby dunking was easier and quicker than bathing the parents. The wee tots, of course, had not been sheared, still, the treatment remained necessary. Those dastardly ticks greedily drank from Megan's animal friends regardless of age. However, after Mojac dipped, no lousy lily-livered little lice lingered long on little lambs. I wonder whether those miserable little sots ever tried sucking on a ... skunk?

-≫   ≪-

Although we rarely lost stock, at times trouble flew in on a dark cloud during a day full of bright sunshine. Have you ever had a youngster come down sick and neither you nor El Medico could figure out the reason? Listen to what happened to one of our just weaned lambs.

One day he was leaping at play. The next day he dragged, moping and dull. Then he stopped eating and drinking. When young animals are in pain they often surrender to it, almost welcoming death. His eyes spoke of pain yet he had no fever. Of most concern to us was his refusal to drink. Newborn lambs often require force feeding. A soft rubber or plastic tube is inserted down the throat into the stomach. You must place your ear at the upper end of that tube as you insert it to be sure the lungs are by-passed. Your tiny lamb is in enough trouble already, no need to add more by puncturing a lung. Mother's milk including the all important colostrum, if the tyke is newborn, can then flow down the tube into baby's stomach, supplying the desperately needed sustenance that can save its life. For this weaned lamb, we were using water. Despite our best efforts, the poor hurting little guy died.

Every method tried, including force-feeding liquids, only worsened the problem and added to his suffering. An autopsy discovered kidney stones, which are quite rare but there they were just the same. In hindsight, we realized it was impossible for him to pass liquid. The more we added, the greater his pain. How sad. How incredibly stupid! We had so much to learn about helping instead of hindering. On a livestock farm, trying to cope with an animal's illness when you, and often the vet, don't know how to help, is truly hard. It leads to many sleepless nights. It leads to self recrimination.

Over the passing years, Mollie-O, Meg and I studied, learned and absorbed much about raising sheep; but, dad blame it, Mojac was never perfect.

6

Meg Meets Sir Francis

A steer gripped by the horn endangers life ... yourn!
Mojac

Every time we thought we'd seen it all, Megan carried and would often pull another arrow from her smarts quiver, which absolutely amazed Mollie-O and me. For example, she'd race full speed up to a woven wire fence, turn her body sideways so as to eel between the strands, and keep right on scooting after recalcitrant sheep. Nobody ever taught her that method; her action was based strictly on instinct. Have I suggested that Megan was a TAG, a talented and gifted, dog? No! Well, stick around; I'll get it out, by and by.

⇥≫ ≪↤

Winter was on the wane our third year when Mojac welcomed a duo of piglets. Durocs by breed, face stuffers by nature. Filet and Mignon were history; however, the food locker was full and so were half our relatives. I am not going to dwell on the demise of our two steers, it is much too depressing. Let me just reemphasize: *Do not make pets of anything planned for placing on your table!* When those two lovable goofs trotted right up to the knacker man to exchange "howdies" on sayonara day, even he was disconcerted. Mollie-O and I bawled our fool heads off!

If Mojac's own beef was superior to the local markets, and it surely was, what about succulent pork? Having acted on that thought, we were now feeding swine. I've used the term "feeding" advisedly, because Packy and Derm ate like two piglets purely determined to make hogs of themselves. Soon, admirably, those pudgy and bulging porkers were close to accomplishing their mission.

Megan was disgusted, especially when the two ignored her efforts to herd them. Piggy devotions ran the gamut from scarfing food to plowing up their paddock — period. A major error occurred when, while still tiny piglets, I failed to ring a couple of noses; I just plain didn't have the heart for it. I've been informed it is the "in" thing with the hip crowd today. Ouch! Piercing any schnoz has to smart a royal bunch. For a human, it must be quite an experience when it comes time for blowing the old honker!

Without being ringed, it was incredible how much earth two inquisitive snouts bulldozed. Paddock grass had no chance to sprout, and the enclosure soon became an arena for the neighbor-hood mud wrestling tournament. In addition, yours truly, unable to enjoy mud free terrain on scenic Mojac Farm, scowled long and often. Neat freak Megan, after tossing me pitying looks, shook the mud off her paws and trotted off to herd the ... ducks! Is it possible I have been tardy in relating about our two fowl-feathered residents?

Two schoolteachers, who'd been labeled "landed gentry", were prime targets to receive their students' cast-off pets. Requests such as: "We thought ... since you have lots of space ... you wouldn't mind ... . Impossible to postpone our vacation ... there's no place we can leave ... so kind of you!"

Accordingly, one year during spring layoff before I could cough up a no, one drake by the name of Sir Francis, and his mate, waddled calmly through Mojac's front gate. I say waddled, because

Sir Francis wasn't knowing how to fly! Megan prepared to explain the house rules, but her new friends were penned up before she had the chance. Ducklings are often used when beginning the sheep dog's training, so it was only natural that Megan would try to schedule a class. Our highest priority, however, was to keep those quackers safe from any opportunistic coyotes roaming the area. Peppy and Megan, if loose, would run them off; nonetheless, easy pickings would be worth the risk for the coyote.

Although I was concerned for their safety, Dame Duck was not. She was a practiced flyer and proved it one day later by bailing out of their pen. Sir Francis was beside himself. Actually, he didn't stop in any one place long enough to be beside himself! With much bobbing to and fro, much quacking and yacking, he cried for the return of the hen. His mate, happily circling, lowered a wing and cruised to a landing back inside the pen.

"So shaddup already! Listen-a-me: run with your big feet, flip-flap both wings, use the air and … fly!" lectured the ace.

Well, make a fan from the fallen feathers, after many beak-bending quackups, and even more three-point landings on his two knees and his nose, Sir Francis, amazingly, cleared the pen fence and — soloed! He became Mojac's Lindbergh.

When drake and mate discovered the pond, they were in webfoot heaven: swimming, flying, buzzing Megan, enjoying their freedom! I, too, enjoy flying, and observing those two Mallard "top-guns" winging through their manual of maneuvers totally delighted me.

Alas, joy was not to last for our flying feathered friends. One drear night a hooded mugger — we think a raccoon — caught the dozing, unaware female. Sir Francis became an act of one. Mojac's Red Baron still flew, still swam, still dive-bombed Her Majesty, but his heart was not in tune. Lonely, he spent hours waddling over pastures searching longingly for the one who wasn't there.

On a beautiful, windy, fall day we watched him glide in to a landing beside the greenhouse. 'Twere blowin' a bloomin' nor'wester gale. Undaunted, his body cored motionless within autumn blow, Mojac's drake, correctly judging the wind's force, and side-slipping perfectly at the last instant, touched down — forgive the old expression — as light as a feather, in that dying storm. Bright, bold sunlight, reflecting in iridescent waves off his neck capped his graceful flight. Truly majestic Sir Francis, flying over Mojac Farm that day, the portrait you printed behind my eyes — never fades.

One week later, a flock of southbound ducks honked noisily over the farm. Sir Francis, quacking loudly, radiated excitement. Taking off, he circled his beloved pond as if to fix it in his mind. Circling once again, slowly this time and quite low over the whole of his farm, our beautiful knight heralded his final farewell and followed his band of brothers into the autumn sky. Sadly, he never blessed Mojac again. Safe flying and happy landings — Sir Francis!

SIR
FRANCIS

By the by, for you long suffering husbands wondering if your wives ever become speechless — learn to *fly!* Although I'd been flying for quite some time, Mollie-O, with an aversion to small planes, had always been reluctant to go climb a cloud with me. One lovely summer day with two hours to kill I suggested a look-see at Mojac Farm from the air. That got her! Of course, Megan begged to go along; however, descending from 2500 feet into the approach leg, an urgent request from a dog to visit the loo can put a decided crimp in the landing. We told her to go bug Peppy and left her home.

The first time Mollie-O's feet left the ground for a prolonged period she did not utter one word, nor open her eyes, from takeoff back to landing, and her death-clutching grasp on the plane's door caused her poor hand to stay cramped for a week. To be sure, 'twas a glorious day! No, of course it didn't last. Having coerced her into another flight, I heard:

"Oh, there's the farm. Isn't it beautiful? Our barns look ever so pretty. You did rototill straight rows in the garden. Look how tall the corn is! I'll bet that's Buttercup leading the flock into the pond pasture. The cross-fencing makes it look so grand. And doesn't the water look simply gorgeous? The wellhouse is so cute. Hi, Meg. Hi, Peppy. Look to the sky, sweeties, here we are way up here! And there, see, our poor ram looks so lonesome in the back pasture. Oh, everything looks simply divine. I just love our little farm! ... "

Yackety-yack, yackety-yack, she chattered like a flaming magpie all the way to the cottony clouds, and back again onto solid macadam!

⇒》 《⇐

Later that fall we had our next bloody crisis. Arriving home from Picture Day at school, a fun-filled festival in itself; on our rounds, Megan discovered that one of the steers had cleverly managed to become one-horned! Mojac had six of the cud-chewers in residence at the time — all unnamed, of course — and I had not been wise enough to poll them while they were young! Drawing inspiration from our rams, the steers occasionally amused themselves by knocking heads. Now half-grown and grain trained, the six would, on call, galumph into the barn, which made it easy to entice the one-horned idiot indoors where I could attempt to effect repairs.

Grannies, was he ever a sight! Blood, still spurting from small veins at the horn's root, dripped everywhere — on him, on me and on Megan. I sent Mollie-O to SOS the vet. What did I know about tying off bleeders? Working the gore-dripping dummy over behind our sheep squeezer, I held him there while waiting for our favorite animal doc to arrive.

The wait was halfway endurable until that knucklehead

stomped on my feet — a stunt he repeated about every five minutes during the day and a half it seemed to take the vet to show up. Between the doc and I, we cauterized, sulfa powdered the stump, and gave One Horn Willy a shot. I really wanted to go get the baseball bat and knock off his other horn, but looking to the future — envisioning steak and a roast or two — I let Megan overrule me.

⇒⟫   ⟪⇐

On a sheep farm, the wee folk, often disguised as "weirdies" drop in for brief visits. I was busy dispersing the last loads of phewey-phewey from barn to ram pasture. Hurrying to finish before the advent of bucket down weather, I wasn't paying much heed to activities elsewhere, until Meg barked to arouse notice. She then led me to one of the lower pastures adjacent to the highway where we had placed our prize ram while his meadow underwent refurbishing. He had recently replaced the five other head bonkers Mojac had been keeping. Culling, a continually necessary pain in the gluteus maximus, is a real bummer. It is most difficult to say good-bye to those you have raised and, loved, but with livestock there is no escape. Stock will only remain strong and healthy with the addition of new blood.

Upon reaching the lower pasture wherein grazed the ram, Megan pointed out his curious and definitely most peculiar behavior. Rather than munching, he was standing before a sturdy oak. As Meg and I watched, he would butt the tree, shake his head and then — you have my word — sigh! I couldn't figure it out. He'd certainly checked out strong and healthy. Closer inspection revealed no wounds, lumps or stings of any kind.

Puzzled, examining the field for clues, I noticed a young couple parked in a car across the highway. Their car radio was on full blast. Suddenly, the answer became clear. Quickly hopping aboard Mojac's old clunker of a tractor, I putt-putted toward the house. Inside, I looted the boom-box from the living room plus a medicinal tape cassette, and chuggy-wheezed back to the pasture where the despondent one continued to dent his — head!

I slapped the tape into the player and soon the pasture air rang with, "There'll Be A Hot Time In The Old Paddock Tonight,"

RamBop stopped bouncing his noggin on the tree and settled back down to chomping Mojac pasture in earnest.

Confused? Have I forgotten to mention that blaring throughout the flaming valley — emanating from the kids' car radio — resounded the ballad, "There Will Never Be Another Ewe!" Remarkable how, once you know the problem, the perfect answer will soothe and heal the troubled.

Gotcha!

BASHFUL RAM

Controlling the expense of livestock feed is an ongoing battle. Not just the successful, but any type of farming is demanding of cost controls. Certainly, percentage between profit and loss on small farms is infinitesimal. Unwatched expenses, especially when turned loose in the ever present game of "credit card roulette" can sneak in and cold-cock the unwary.

That fall, Mojac approached grain feeding costs in a different manner. My parents rented pasture on their valley farm to a local dairyman and as feed for his cattle he had planted corn that year. Mollie-O, Megan and I arranged for a pickup load of silage as part payment for land rental. Our Dodge pickup came with a set of wooden, portable, stock racks, which I installed whenever transporting Mojac's animals or when purchasing others. Those tall racks added considerable depth to the truck's carrying space.

After school on one of Oregon's renowned fall days, racks aboard, we drove our one-lunged cougher to the valley, met the farmer and soon bounced beside his tractor through the corn field as his machinery chopped the crop, stalks and all, and spit it from a spout-like chute into our truck bed. Before Megan could bark three times, the pickup brimmed full and we were ready to roll.

A stop at the local market to purchase heavy duty plastic bags, then on up the hill and home. Driving the Dodge through the opened orchard gate, I parked in the paddock next to the sheep barn. Mollie-O and I flew to the house, changed into grubbies and huffy-puffed back to the barn. Greeting the sheep, we fed and watered. Phew! Now to perform a typical Mojac task — the hard way.

Wrap hands around a shovel, dig that handy dandy tool into the corn, fill a plastic sack, then tie its big mouth shut. Settling silage is inclined to heat up, which reminded me of the classic rhyme:

"Fire, fire," sez Mrs. Maguire.

"Where, where?" sez Mrs. Blair.

"The sheep barn," sez Mrs. Shelarn.

"God save us," sez Mrs. Davis.

After stuffing half the Willamette Valley's corn crop into plastic bags, we stored all the sacks outdoors in a paddock inaccessible to sheep. Next, hose out the not altogether unpleasant smelling residue from the Dodge. Then, as it's not burning daylight yet, we'll stagger up to the house, feed Meg, grab a bite ourselves and step out again onto the patio in time to catch the sunrise. We thumbed our noses at Old Man Winter that year, because, like

Oregon beavers, Mojac is now ready for that eyebrow frosting, tail freezing, squinty-eyed runt!

Although bags were tightly tied, the wafting aroma across the paddock was intoxicating. I'll be durned if that settling silage hadn't turned each one of those sacks into corn squeezin's! Megan, Mollie-O and I soon concluded that our barn mice had gone round the twist. Those tiny twits had chewed holes in half the plastic sack bottoms ... and gorged! After which they stood atop wooden gates weaving, laughing uproariously and waving their tails tantalizingly at the cats. Fortunately for them those same wind-clued kitties had sniffed, found those bags containing the secret for permanent feline youth, and also pie-eyed, were unaware of the soused rodents insulting actions.

Mojac's always courteous sheep threw good manners out the barn door in eager haste to dive into such fine smelling tasty grub. Quietly reposing after their gourmet dining, benevolent expressions outlining character on woolly faces, and with an occasional "excuse me" burp, the flock lazed contentedly.

While we might have had a question or two regarding nutritional value of corn silage versus mixed grain, there is no doubt that all Mojac's animals that winter summed up by being benign kids. Even our young rams extended the foreleg fraternal sign of brotherhood, instead of denting craniums!

Was silage a good choice of feed that year? For sure the price paged out in the black. If deciding from the animals viewpoint, the questions been answered.

Not to worry, our lamb crop turned out to be all *teetotalers*.

⇒⟩ ⟨⇐

I've mentioned that a raccoon, perhaps, caught Sir Francis's mate. It might also have been a coyote. Not long after our sheep dipping festival, I spotted an early morning forager padding his cautious way from Megan's pond pasture towards the barn. I grabbed my old "blam and blast 'em" off its peg and eeled quietly out the back door. Imitating my favorite childhood Indian hero, Chingachgook, and carefully clutching Your Demise, I moccasined lightly past the wellhouse proceeding to stalk the stalker. Ha! This

Mojac brave couldn't stalk diddley squat. If that alert four-footed coyote bandit had been Magua, warrior chief of the Hurons, and the Mohicans nemesis, my already sparse scalp would soon have been gracing a pole in his lodge!

I had absolutely no intention of sending that soft walking trespasser to howl among the angels. Nonetheless, a loud bang reverberating in a perked ear might induce him to change his thieving mind about tasty snacking on succulent Mojac lamb. With the possible exception of all tax assessors, once I'd reached mature age, I've never wanted to shoot anything or anyone.

This Mohican had clumsy feet, probably along with bad breath. Coyote heard me, smelled me, saw me and farewelled me. A swift whirl and the thief was hot-footing back from whence he'd come. He was truly a fine looking animal. I took a bead and fired over his head anyway. It couldn't hurt he should hurry!

Coyotes are not admired by livestock raisers, and make no mistake, a coyote will — kill! They can absolutely devastate a sheep flock. Nevertheless, I admired this one. Attentive to Your Demise's oral "howdy", he shifted from canter to gallop. Sailing high over five, four-foot, electrified wire field fences, he calmly, effortlessly and floatingly made it look so easy I had to applaud. One final saucy flick of his tail and coyote was gone. I bet the farm you too would have enjoyed the view of that survivor displaying his superb skills. Surely a grand sight to recall: a day, a week, a month, a year later. Of course, I can say all this because Mojac lost nary a lamb to coyotes during our ten years with sheep.

FLYING COYOTE

7

Meg and Snow, Snow, Snow

A frog when he copes ... croaks!

Mojac

Border collies are not only mannerly — they're exception-
ally clean — leaning to the fastidious. Yet, I must confess to
puzzlements. Rain-wet or pond-wet, Megan carefully licked
herself dry like a tabby. Her fur thus donned the impeccable.
Dunk her in a bath, and drip-dried, combed, ribbon be-decked,
Magoo promptly face plowed into the closest phewey-phewey
pile, rolled, grinned and licked her bod from smelly end to smelly
end. What did I know? Well, for one thing her goodnight kiss was
definitely — out!

Megan's good manners displayed best padding before society,
especially when at local sheep trials. Megan never competed. Her
training had never been completed because I lacked the time and
was never close to being good enough anyway; however, together
with Mollie-O, Dave and I, she always enjoyed watching herders,
dogs and woollies work.

All Borders are well behaved at sheep trials. Eager to participate, they are self-restrained bystanders when others work. Time clocks being their major enemies, those trials are terribly hard on the dogs. Frequently, working against that accursed clock, upon completing their gathering and then retiring from the field, they would be so hot, immersing in a water tank became an immediate requirement in order to avoid dehydration and ... even death!

Barking is one huge no-no at these exhibitions. Border collies maintained silence, most other breeds did not. Spectators often elected to bring pets to sheep trials, everything from tiny Chihuahuas to Great Danes. Immediately, loud, ill-mannered canine opinions would then interrupt the serious business of the day. In accord and almost in unison, herders and Borders alike would turn, stare at the offenders, elevate their noses and privately utter — Peasants!

At one trial, visitors piloting a whole pickup load of Irish Setters, incessant mouthers, rolled in, parked, received irate stares, cranked back up and hit the bricks. Shepherds eyeballed one another, grinned and inwardly voiced, "By grab and hallelujah — the flaming neighborhood's been saved one more time!"

Mojac looked forward to those farm escapes. Mollie-O always packed a sheepman's gourmet lunch: baked chicken, cheese, French breads, fruit, and wine — crisp and chilled. The eating was great and the dogs superb — a delight to watch. Comfortably ensconced in our take along folding sitters, Ol' Sol warming the carcass, eyes full of Borders plus sheep, stomachs paunching from Molly's super grits, and owners of the world's finest Border Collie. Hey, looky here, our cups up and ranneth over. Dear Phantasus, those dreamy days were real and I loved them!

Much can louse up a trial: an over warm day, recalcitrant woollies, tired dogs, over zealous herders, way too many signals (whistled or voiced) and — bad luck. When it does go wrong, viewers also ache. On the other hand, a superb performance and winners' pride — dog's and shepherd's — also decorates your face.

Some towns in our area combine sheep trials with a variety of other activities: crafts, weavings, sheep shearing lessons and juicy lamb burgers hot off the grill. They are fun and best of all uncrowded, which beats the pants off watching some yo-yo at a rock concert, busily chewing on a live chipmunk, prance half naked across a stage while discordantly strumming a guitar into a nervous breakdown. Scratching an itch, wherever located — like Bonzo the chimpo — he squalls repulsive obscenities into a cringing microphone. His claim to fame is an Ode to Barf!

By contrast, sheep trials and small town fairs are low key, laid back, neighborly and quiet; homey and oh so comfortable. I purely do thank thee, Lord!

Speaking of lunch. Any more of that chicken, maybe a smidgen of bread and cheese and a wee cold drop of that wine — Mollie-O darlin'? Davey, Megan and meself are fast fadin' away to shadders.

⇒》　《⇐

I hate flies! Those miserable, pesky, tormenting insects make the lives of animals, especially cattle, intolerable. Mean, disgraceful treatment of livestock is also one of my pet peeves. Not just filthy barns, stale water and inadequate feed, but lack of protection against flies. That need not be! With a little ingenuity, a powder sack and some grain, those nasty little rotters can be thwarted. Mollie-O and I installed a portable chute, wide enough for one steer at a time to pass, in the entryway to their barn and blocked off the rest of the opening. I bought a sack of special dusting powder, which, for want of the correct name, I shall call Fly Buzz Off. When bumped or struck, the bag emitted a generous dusting of fine powder. We suspended the sack over the midway point of the chute, just low enough to conk One Horn Willy and his pals on the mush when they passed.

After covering the bottom of the indoor feeder with grain, I sent Megan off to herd Big Stoop and his troops into the barn paddock. Layering the bottom of an old bucket with additional bovine bait and then thumping on it, I hollered to entice them into the narrow opening of the chute. Those gut-stuffing dogies would purely waltz for an extra tiffin. Continuing to belt my pail, I yodeled, "Yoo-hoo, Klutz and Company, come to papa, I'm handing out bon-bons."

Willy boy needed no further urging. He came tracking up to the chute opening like a runaway train. Tracking, that is, until he spied the dust sack. Immediately, he yanked the emergency cord and screeched to a rail-smoking halt! Meanwhile, beating a tune on the bucket like a Yankee Doodle drummer, I backed my easily bruised bod into the chute in front of him, showing him the grain. With his silly grin and single horn, Willy looked a lot dumber than he was. He knew what was in the barn feeder, and also the bucket. He wanted both. One more dulcet yodel from the bucket thumper, another — whoa! This time though, Cautious tracked deeper into the chute, and further on each of my succeeding pleas. Finally, Willy gave the sack serious study. Calculating that if he couldn't dodge that breeze blowing pest, he would try to kill it. El Toro — the brave — advanced, hooked that varmint with his one remaining horn, passed on under and struck gold in his feed trough!

When the sack flew up and over his head, landing on his hind end, Willy was coated from nose to tail with such a lovely dusting of Fly Buzz Off.

One by one, in between grain replenishments, Willy's gang followed the leader. Once all grits had been licked clean, the program "Dust 'em," repeated with more powder puffing on the way out — this time with less shying, snorting and swearing.

Mojac counted it a well earned eye-filling pleasure seeing their cattle peacefully browsing without a dirty disease carrying mass of flies, buzzing, congesting, and swarming around their eyes, ears and noses. We could never understand why the dusting program wasn't universal on all farms. Certainly, given the return, it wasn't difficult or expensive to implement.

⇒⇒   ⇐⇐

After nearly destroying ourselves renovating the pond, Mojac wondered if the wild Hill creatures would also enjoy our improvements. Megan, we already knew, approved, as did Sir Francis and mate. Mother Nature, by sending a chorus of frogs to take up residence along the shallow banks, didn't take long to reward our efforts. For six weeks, beginning early each spring, Le Croakaire du Pond would delight our ears with a full-blown nightly opera. La

Traviata in froggie profundo. Delighted doesn't express our joy. Throughout our more than ten years, those Carnegie Hall performances serenaded Mojac Farm, free of charge and far into the night. As we listened in rapt appreciation to many favorite arias, bent backs didn't complain quite as loudly and flaming calluses didn't burn hot, at least, not as often!

⇒≫   ≪⇐

One year, two weeks prior to the advent of fall breeding, ever vigilant Megan noticed that our only ram, a prize breeder, seemed under the weather. El Papa, a purebred Suffolk, had been producing big, handsome, Mojac lambs. Talking him into sick call, she tenderly escorted him into our barn patch and repair quarters. Inspection revealed an abscess on the right side of his jaw. I cleaned and cauterized the inflammation as thoroughly as he'd allow, then injected his backside with a shot of penicillin to ward off further infection. Promising Megan I would keep an eye on him, I returned the big guy to pasture and continued with my daily chores.

I've already referred to culling, so you know that maintaining healthy stock and producing future champions requires changing bloodlines — often. Mother could breed to son and father to daughter, beyond that was not advisable.

Our investment in El Papa was considerable; thus, two days later and keeping my word to Meg, Pops was back for another office visit. His infected jaw was not healing. Upon further brief inspection, it appeared to me to be an impacted tooth. I would be allowed to shove my thumb in his mouth, but Dad surely wasn't going to hold it open long enough for this dummy to poke around in there. Mollie-O headed off to the telephone.

Waiting for the vet, Megan and I argued at length about the merits of city dude sheep farming. Her Border collie logic, as usual, rang me up loser ... again!

Once arrived and after further inspection, Doc's diagnosis agreed with mine. When the ram remained close-mouthed, determined to resist treatment, the vet decided on a light shot of knockout drops. Meg directed, I held Papa and Doc needled our ram to sleep.

El Papa now comatose, dreaming of alfalfa and grain, Doc and I propped open his chompers for a thorough examination. The vet probed, disinfected, cleaned and swabbed. He could not find one sad, sorry, blamed thing wrong! Papa's mouth was the answer to any dentist's prayer, better make that a patient's prayer, a "painless puller" wouldn't have made a dime on that mouth.

While Pops grabbed some post trauma zees, propped up between a couple of hay bales, Mollie-O, Doc and I headed to the house for coffee. Meg was too young for a cup of java so I dipped her dog bone in mine. We enjoyed visiting with the vet and swapping lies. If any animal needed treatment, never mind conditions or hour, he would always come. Mojac respected him for that, and we also truly enjoyed his company.

After a suitable time trying to top one another's war stories, the three of us and Meg headed down to the emergency ward to check on Rip Van Winkle. Upon entering the barn our vision told us the ram was still in the Land of Nod. Or was he?

Damn and blast! Closer inspection revealed not a snoozing patient, but a dead ram! The minor amount of "beddy-bye" in the shot had been too much for the heart of Mojac's sheep dad of the year.

Later, when the shock, coupled with roiling waves of panic, began to subside, the one we felt sorriest for was Doc. Terribly upset, he blamed himself, which was really unfair. We had always known that a level of risk attends the decision to put someone — human or animal — temporarily to sleep. Weight and age are only a couple of factors to consider when estimating dosage. In this case, there was no fault to find.

Reassuring the vet, and sending him on his way, I glumly loaded our poor Pops on Cuthbert, our tractor trailer, and carried his body to the instrument shed, there to await the hastily called knacker man.

Ever have a sinking — spinning into the void — kind of dream? Like one where you're sitting comfy on the front porch swing, after dinner, when a strong gust of wind playfully shoves it out over the Grand Canyon? Startled, staring upward, you notice both ropes have begun to fray, and all you can think about is the extra helping of chicken legs you pigged out on at supper. Afraid to eye-ball those parting strands again, you wonder how long until the swing lets go and your chunky bod drops into the Colorado? In sheer panic you quickly blink-a-blink, hoping to wake up and end the nightmare.

Unfortunately, our dead ram was no dream. Standing, staring down at him, I knew we were in trouble. Mojac money being abundant — as plentiful as free samples from a bank — what to do? Alfalfa, needed winter feed, had almost doubled in price, and grain, making a matched pair of runaways, kept pace. Our tax-fat government piously assured those who foot its bills that "Inflation was under control." Oh, sure, and I'll bet, if you water it — wildflowers will bloom in the cat's box — too!

How do spring lambs arrive sans help of willing ram? I hadn't a flaming clue. Ruminating about the lack of a living ruminant sire, one thought kept repeating, Mojac, up to our eyeballs in debt and with no spare money, simply could not afford another expensive ram this year.

Sad, lacking a solution, we finished nightly tasks and trudged wearily off to bed. Sleep turned nocturnal as my thoughts continued to whirl. Dawn was yawning when a notion finally tantalized my weary brain — then registered, retreated, returned — and locked in. Pastured with our market wethers were two promising young lambs I had not castrated. Doubtful at first I dismissed the idea because neither lamb was yet six months old. One, with a roving eye, was a good looking broth of a ram. Of course, wishin' ain't fishin', but Mojac didn't have a whole lot of other choices.

Two weeks later, all ewes happily flushed, our fingers tightly crossed, we watched as Shorty hoppy-skipped over the bridge, through the gate and into the pasture we'd named Ewe Happy Land. That little sucker sashayed across the meadow like a kitten who had just fallen out of his tree and landed in a wagon load of catnip!

⇥⇥⇥   ⇤⇤⇤

Vacating a warm bed, especially in the dark on a cold winter morning, is totally uncivilized! Naturally, Megan — that nauseating cur — bounced cheerfully out of the sack every flaming, frigid morning, bright eyed and raring to go. "Let's move your plodders, slowpoke," she would yip excitedly, grating my surly nerves as I shivered my way to the barn in the gloom of those crisp snowy mornings. Every crunching foot of the way she performed the Megan gambado.

Though I was confident our Megan was canine, I confronted doubts when a fresh snowfall turned her into a seal. Diving headfirst into the nearest drift, she would disappear, using her legs as flippers, only to resurface a few yards away blowing like a porpoise. To say that Magoo savored winter's icy blanket would be a gross understatement; she positively reveled when her nose became coated with the cold white fluff! Reminiscent of her unending forays into her pond, Megan's enjoyment of the snow lasted for ages, long after Ma and Pa retired inside to defrost their frozen noses in front of a warm fire.

CANINE
SNOWBALL

Snow on Mojac Farm? You can honk your horn if I lie! Blizzardy and three feet or more? Amen, brother! Experience difficulty breaking trail to the barn to feed, thaw water and check stock? Naw. Tiddly fun! Descending from iced hills, happily sliding to school, was that perhaps hazardous? Quite often, words failed me along with my nerves! How long were we blessed with, o' lordy me, great depths of that cheek numbing stuff? How long is forever? Nevertheless, you'd purely have to strain to hear us complain. All Mollie-O had to mezzo was, "Be-deep, be-deep, oh hush, be-deep," and I knew the warmth of March along with our frogs would soon arrive, freeing sun and melting snow.

Surviving that long, uncertain winter with but minor catastrophes, Mojac, apprehensive, was truly ready to welcome spring's budding and birthing.

With their woolly winter coats and bellies fat from winter feed, it wasn't easy to tell if our ewes were in the family way. Ever the pessimist, I still entertained strong doubts about Shorty's abilities, he'd been such a little guy way back there in the fall!

Fingers numbly crossed, we harkened when Le frogs sang of good tidings. Contented ewes rattled their paddock gate with impatient noses, eager to return to pasture. Yes! It was spring. That Oregon stranger — warming sun — shone. Could the wonder and joy of lambing be far away? How fervently we hoped bankruptcy would not blossom with the daffodils.

You won't be surprised to learn, little Shorty had definitely taken care of business. All of his ladies gave birth. Most to twins, some to triplets. Nary one lamb was lost and there wasn't a single, lonely, sad little bummer in the crowd. Just like that, Shorty boy was now our big, proud, handsome, bragging — Mojac sire. Molly and I smiled at one another, able now to relax for the first time since, months ago, we'd crossed our fingers.

Megan skylarked all over the pastures woofing, "I told you so, I told you so."

"Bestoweth our champion a proper name," trilled Mollie-O. "A ewe favored beau such as he deserves an appropriate title."

"No problem," bubbled I. "That happy deed hast already been accomplished. Now and forever more — oh champion of Mojac — thy name, E. FLYNN, (after Errol ... who else?) shall ring forth from these blessed and sacred Hills."

To our delight, E. Flynn proved to be our superior ram papa for many years. His offspring all grew straight, tall and strong. *Au grand sérieux,* our swaggering swain sweet-talked every ewe he ever met into a sheepish stroll down lover's lane — and they giggled all the way back!

8

Meg and Buttercup

A lamb in the house ... say good-bye to your spouse!
Mojac

Considering our frantic and hectic pace during the early years, Mollie-O and Megan, in that order, unquestionably kept the wheels from falling off the wagon. Not only did my spouse perform domestic chores, she also helped me with the slugging tasks around the farm. Storing twine-wrapped hay bales in the barn was hot, sweaty, dusty, dirty, tiring work, but not backbreaking. Nor was it difficult loading the tractor with those feathery fifty pound delights. But you haven't worked until you've dragged heavy, three-strand wire bales of alfalfa up twenty stair treads into a barn loft for winter storage? Mojac did! Call us fools, but it was the only way Mollie-O and I could slug-haul the lung-collapsing killers up there. Care to try it with forty bales?

Alfred, our old chugger of a tractor, was a 1950 Cub Farmall — fine in its heyday, but a tad ancient by 1978. Nevertheless, I used it for almost all farm tasks, including those I invented.

Unfortunately, a pulley arrangement mounted over the barn door and used for hoisting wasn't sturdy enough to handle large bales of heavy alfalfa. Alfred became a ninety pound weakling when wrestling those heavies, thus it necessitated yo-ho-ho time, and broke the backs of the two who were dumb enough to buy the farm in the first place! Thinking about it today my back starts moaning all over again.

⇛   ⇚

'Twas truly Mollie-O who formed Mojac into a functioning operation. Meg and I owed her a ton, which explains why we built her a beach house after leaving the farm. But that's another story.

⇛   ⇚

Megan, for her part, always tried to dislocate her hind end when greeting us. Work proud, eager to learn and full of life she could make those occasional tough days — striving with non-receptive young minds — disappear straight up that proverbial smokestack. Actually, Megan was almost capable of managing Mojac Farm all by herself. She oversaw feeding and watering of stock, weaning of lambs, shearing, clipping and docking, as well as herding, haying, forking, loading, and dumping phewey-phewey. Megan even knew the routine we followed when toting lambs to market. Because this is an honest narrative, I must report she became stymied when called upon to repair the power takeoff and change cutter blades on Alfred. I know you can't wait to whisper in my ear that Megan was a dog! Biologically, yes, yet she was more human than a whole passel of the two legged kind. Further, explain if you can, how the one with such a formidable intellect, our advice giver, that smidgen, no account, four-legged lover, still softly pads the forest trails of my mind on a daily basis!

⇛   ⇚

I seem to remember already relating my chicken-hearted failure to ring the pigs' noses. We paid for that twice, in a destroyed paddock and in an episode that though kind of funny could have turned out tragic. It happened this way: Megan, Mollie-O and I had once again talked my parents into farm critter sitting, and the three of us had tootled away to the friendly sea, where, in those peaceful days, no noisy crowds or traffic jams irked us. Keiko was still flipping over Spanish!

⇒⟫ ⟪⇐

When Mojac arrived home after a rejuvenating two days, my mother reported that one of the pigs had rooted himself under the wooden feeder in his pen and she hadn't been able to entice him out. Packy and Derm bulged midsize by then and it was too difficult for the elderly to haul and topside him. Older than dirt myself now, I fully understand dilemmas such as those.

I beat feet quickly to the porker's pen. Sure enough there was Big Derm wedged on his side under the slatted board feeder. He had submarined his fool self three-quarters of the way under the trough, which was securely fastened to the back wall of their shelter.

Bending way over, I grabbed hold of his hind legs, and with a mighty heave — complete with three torn ligaments and an apt swearword — hauled the lummox out. Derm must have been trapped for about thirty-six hours without food or water. When he first regained his feet, he staggered and lurched around like a snockered Skidrow resident, and he was only too happy to shove his snout in a bucket of water. Shaking and sloshing, he then hobbled to the grit trough and inhaled! During that gorging eternity I worried he wouldn't raise his bugler long enough to swallow. Saved him we did, but it was close. A few more hours could have seen lardy Derm off to piggy heaven. And later, after his sandhogging weekend, he never did catch up to Packy in size or weight. Dressed out, Slim weighed thirty-five pounds less than his buddy. Oh well, it isn't the amount of the bacon in the pig, it's the quality of the bacon in the man!

⇒⟫ ⟪⇐

As the years advanced, Mollie-O and I finally figured out that winter lambing for a couple of teachers cum sheep raisers was too exhausting. Hours of study, constant reference to The Shepherd, a wonderful magazine, beaucoup trial and error, and a modicum of ram-ewe cooperation, we learned that we could predict our new lambs' birthdays within a two week span and with ninety percent accuracy. How do you like them apples?

Armed with this new sense of control, we decided to try to coordinate the magic time for Mojac during Spring Layoff. Mollie-O and I figured we could go for a week at school without sleep, but certainly not two. Our first day back would usually find us leaning against a lot of doors! Lambing like this kept Mojac Farm busier than a school of friendly piranha practicing subtraction on your toes. It was a week of early to rise and never to bed, hold me up mother, I think I'm dead.

Entering the barn one particular morning, Mojac stepped into pandemonium. Mamas and their lambs were everywhere, keening, cleaning, calling and bawling. Overnight, we had reaped a baby birth bonanza — a veritable mother load! Mollie-O and I fetched, carried and matched well into the next century. After pairing, milking, jugging and latching, we cast final looks around the barn to count the older nursing lambs and also the still pregnant ewes. A separated, new born lamb and mother ewe would not bode well for the baby.

WHO BE'S THAT?

Mollie-O

Perhaps a clearer picture of the barn layout would help: About twenty feet wide and thirty deep, the wood structure supporting a hip style metal roof, faced north. A further fifteen feet of width had been added to form the maternity section. The metal roof on this addition sloped, tying on to the loft floor a touch below the eaves. Three telephone-pole-circumference logs one quarter way in on each side of the main room, counting up six, and running north to south, supported the loft floor. Fifteen feet above that upper level was the barn roof.

Creep, loft stairs and suspended grinder feed box were located on the west side. In between, and fastened to the three poles on the east side, a plywood, cone-shaped hay feeder had been installed. It had been built with an open gap on the bottom which allowed eager mouths to pull forth hay. The grain tray, fastened eighteen inches below the gap, ran the full length of the feeder. This most serviceable joining of tray and feeder protruded equally into main barn and Maternity Row, thus dining was accomplished from both sides. When the need arose, jugs were assembled and placed along Maternity's east wall.

The north gate was the primary entrance. Here I had poured a steel reinforced, eleven by twelve-foot — four-inch thick — concrete slab to keep mud outdoors. I did the same at the northeast gate leading to Maternity Row. The seldom-used south entrance required no slab, but its sliding, metal-covered door allowed for air circulation during warm weather and protection from the elements during winter and spring. The north and Maternity Row gates always remained open to the Hill climate.

The main barn and maternity side were separated by a wide, dutch door. All expectant mothers deserve some privacy. That door could also be fastened open to allow mothers and weaned lambs free use of both sides of the feeder after all ewes had delivered.

A necessary faucet-fed water tub was located just inside to the right of the north gate, in the corner of the main barn beside the dutch door. Feed room, containing Meg's hidey-hole, and waiting room have already been described.

To continue with chaos morning: After we had checked all of the nursing babes, I thought I heard another soft bleat. Sure enough, away off in a dark corner, repeated lonesome baaing led us to an unclaimed lambkin. Two woeful eyes and another plaintive little cry greeted us. Once in a while, the shepherd becomes a foster parent to a bummer. A bummer is a tyke who has been rejected by its biological mother for reasons clear only to her. Sometimes when the true mother bawls, "nay," to her baby, if you are lucky you can fool another ewe into accepting the orphan.

Why will ewes reject their own lambs? Good question. Mojac figured the reasons ranged from: "Read my lips, Mac. My contract clearly states, one baby only. Two lambs I have and one is all I'm going to keep. So, why don't you and Little Bo Peep over there, shove off!" Frequently, she is a young ewe experiencing a first birth; she becomes excited, often confused. When twins are produced momma may move away from her firstborn in order to deliver the second; in the interim, numero uno can be totally forgotten; after all, she thought her problem was traceable to an upset stomach! It often rains in Oregon, a peal of thunder might have frightened the new mother, causing her to take a hike to the other end of the barn. As Mojac kept wary eyes peeled for those kinds of incidents rejection won't take place if we are present during the blessed event.

And finally: Unhappy, hindsight her instructor, the new mother now wishes she'd pleaded a headache and sent Big Beau over to visit her sister!

Regardless, Woeful's plight exists and it is up to you to find a solution.

The reasons for bummers stack high, solutions unlayer but few: Methods to try merging lamb with a mother list plentiful, maybe a new one will work. Chances are, after three fast ones over the plate, you'll probably strike out.

First of all, the reluctant ewe has to be one of those you have jugged; they are the only ones to have just given birth. It will likely be a momma with a single lamb. Triplets do arrive, but they are rare. Therefore, you can usually eliminate ewes with twins.

On paydirt morning, we had housed seven ewes and twelve lambs on Maternity Row. Five of the mothers were proudly singing to twins, which narrowed the possibilities to the two crooners with singles — maybe. Remember, ewes can also birth triplets.

Pitch number one: We'll carry little woeful eyes over to a jugged mother with a single and place the baby inside her pen. If momma is the one, will she now be willing to accept her lamb? Perhaps the gods smile and Mom will cry, "Where have you been tiny tot lambkin? I just about gave up on you." Oh, joy, happiness abounds, the long lost has been found and this family just increased by one.

However, this coy mother bent over, sniffed Big Eyes and bawled, "No way! You're not mine, get lost!" Then she tried to butt the orphan through the slats of her jug. Observe our newborn baby folks: Maybe two to three hours old, she is still wobbly on her pins. Lots of rude things have already beset her. She'd been needled, iodined, squeezed and — bashed! Welcome, is definitely not woven into her blanket. No lovin' hug, no comfort, no warmth, no food. What has Little Orphan Annie done that's so wrong? I could go on but you're way ahead of me interpreting this picture. Strike one! Big Butter never even looked at the ball.

Pitch number two: We'll milk Belting Bertha, smear her milk on poor Woeful and try the ewe again. PATOOEY! Strike two! Our poor baby struggled back on to its feet and wobbled weakly across the jug. Our mother had watched a curve float by and never blinked an eye.

Pitch number three: We restrict Mom's movement in the pen so she cannot butt baby, and then tie one of her rear legs to a jug slat to curtail stomping. Now, in appearance, she resembles a trussed turkey. We'll insert our orphan in the pen once more and leave the family alone for about an hour. During that time, Woeful will at least latch onto a faucet for a quick pick-me-up. Returning quietly, we released the turkey. BAM! Baaing butted baby bounces back off the jug slats one more time. Strike three! This butter is out!

Cross that ewe off the list and repeat the procedure with single mother number two. When the other ewe struck out you probably heard me using some bad words.

Are there more ideas for outwitting obdurate ewes? Yes. I have rubbed Bag Balm on adult's nose and baby's body, no question they smelled alike then. No luck. Long time sheepmen insist they have a never fail solution. Find a ewe with a dead lamb, skin the carcass, tie the pelt around your bummer and set the baby

up on the bereaved mother's teat. Two gulps and a swallow and —
presto — huzzahs to another happy new family. Mojac took extra
good care of their flock, consequently, our newborn lambs rarely
died. We had no stillborns on that day.

Early on in the sheep business, an emphatic statement from
Mollie-O:

"Look you, boyo. Not one single, solitary, individual, lone
lamb will I have in my house and that's FINAL!"

Mojac took Buttercup — formerly Woeful — up and into the
house. Mollie-O and Meg bottle fed, diapered (cross my heart),
cuddled and loved her. (There was no way we could leave our
orphan on her own down in that barn. Truly unwanted she would
have had to sneak behind ewes feeding at the big trough and, going
from one to another, try to grab a quick mouthful. Offended
mothers would have happily, in turn, airmailed the hungry waif
across the barn!)

I have a photo of Mollie-O, one of my favorites. The proxy
mom half-reclines on the living room sofa. Buttercup, diapered and
snug in a blanket, reposes on her adopted parent's chest. Megan is
lying on Mollie-O's slippers. All three are totally zonked. The title?
"Position in Life is Everything." So much for a lamb in the flaming
house!

More than one lamb took up residence in the house and
whenever one of them was bottle feeding on a lap, Megan would
walk over, lie down in front, rest her chin on a boot and stare up at
the feeder, her eyes saying, "Take good care of that kid; the little
twit is one of mine." Meg protected her Buttercup like the lamb was
one of the pups she'd never had.

Mojac's Buttercup became the sweetest ewe we ever raised
— without peer as a mother. With E. Flynn's willing help, she
produced three sets of triplets and two sets of twins in five years.
Her lambs were raised on love. Bummer, that despised term, never
crossed her lips. Buttercup was Mojac's best Suffolk; in her own
way, the equal of Megan. And you know how good she had to be to
accomplish that.

Buttercup thrived in her new quarters, especially the very
personal TLC from Meg, Mollie-O, Dave and me. Our Dave took
over the baby-sitting duties while Molly and I were away at school.

When not being bottle fed on his lap, they would stroll the farm. Dave called those explorations his Recruit Lamb Indoctrination course. Marines never get out of the habit of reconnoitering. Buttercup soon learned every foot of Mojac Farm, including Megan's pond. Dave even took her to town on his daily shopping forays. Thank God he never introduced her to hamburgers!

Peppy looked forward to scouting the terrain, too. With Dave in attendance on the farm, he could be freed from his pen to engage in some serious exercise, and he loved the extra freedom allotted to him to challenge the wind. The only problem for Li'l Butter with him was that when he licked her, he knocked her down.

Squeaky took to Buttercup right off; the lamb didn't try to steal his milk, neither did she make any attempt to grab his tail, so he chalked her up as harmless and friendly. He even went far enough overboard to lick her face, too, and for Boss Squeaky that was indeed acceptance. All in all, even though she'd been unwanted, our orphan lamb had to be enjoying babyhood.

MEG AND
BUTTERCUP

9

Meg and Peppy's Socks

Even for a Buttercup, life can be a ... bummer!

Mojac

I've mentioned how our school children's parents would often ask Mojac to board their little sneezer's pets. Farm visits with toddlers in tow for close-up animal viewing were also requested. Megan had no quarrel with that as it gave her a chance to show off. We also endorsed those visitations for — when youngsters become better acquainted with the care and raising of domestic animals — less time is wasted on television's inanities.

Buttercup grew into a charming, gentle ewe with a friendly disposition much like Megan's. One quick example will demonstrate what I mean:

One day after Li'l Butter was full grown and had become a mother in her own right, Mollie-O received a request from a parent of one of her students to visit Mojac Farm for a family "Dr. Doolittle Day." (Somebody must have told them we had a Pushmi-Pullyu hidden in the barn.) Mollie-O had agreed with the proviso

— as we would be away stock buying — our guests must ensure that all gates were closed and secured behind them; a premature tête-á-tête between E. Flynn and his ladies we did not need!

Mollie-O also informed the mother that if, upon entering the pond pasture, she were to call, "BUTTERCUP," Mojac's pride and joy might trot over and share some scintillating sheep salutations with one and all. When our guest's husband heard these instructions, he said, "You've got to be off your rocker. You mean to tell me that the whole family can tippy-toe into a pasture full of sheep, holler 'BUTTERCUP', and one of those woolies will hootie-tootie over and chew the cud with us? I have really got to see that!"

You know the rest of the story. Visitors performed as directed. Buttercup, our true champion, trotted right over and extended her famous Mojac welcome. According to neighborhood gossip, minutes later the husband totally unnerved by the whole experience tripped and fell into a pile of phewey-phewey! His wife, when she finally quit laughing, recited the following:

"He has camped through the Wallowas just having a ball,
Hunting for Bighorn late in the fall.
Adventures he's had; oh, yes, quite a few,
But he's never before been kissed by a — ewe!"

As for Mojac, we can but wish the joy of a Buttercup for you, when coping with all your — bummers!

Mollie-O

HEY, MA, WE CAN'T
REACH IT

⇒≫   ≪⇐

Surprisingly, it was easy to train lambs to the creep. Entering their barn for dinner and eager for Mom's kind of grits, our thriving babies still couldn't reach the adult feed trough.

Mojac benefited. The babies were now at the half-way point of the Mojac process: beginning to wean and being fully weaned. Curious about the smell of grain, as they stood beside feeding mothers, we could quietly grab the little ones and shove them, one by one, through the opening in the creep door. Remember, that entrance was only large enough for lambs to enter, it was far too small for ewes.

Because of the creep, transition went smoothly for lambs introduction to grain, but their new feeding station created loud global bellyaching. Babies, now separated from Mom, yelled for help. After much hither, much yon, much baaing, much bawling — much ado about nothing — one of the hithers, sniffed the laid out grain placed in a feeder exactly suited to a lamb's height — imagine that!

"Look guys," the sniffer hollered. "Some yummy molasses-coated chocolate-chip cookies." The stampede was on, followed by much face stuffing — and soon peace and sweet silence would envelop the creep.

Uh-oh! The now sated ewes have sighted their missing lambs but cannot stuff their big bods through the creep door. More belly-aching, mom and lamb in discordant chorus. A pitiful Mojac wail to all the saints. Ding-blast! Most times, raising sheep was one grand and glorious — *bellyache!*

Our little squirts now chewing grain and alfalfa would still bug mater for milk as a chaser. A rumor had circulated among the lambs that butting Mom would increase her milk flow. Additionally, two belts are always better than one, and the further mother rises off the ground the greater the flow of nectar.

Well, naturally, Momma soon grew tired of all that tummy-thumping jazz because, the bigger her lamb the higher she flew. Finally, when Mom began to resemble a helicopter experiencing a crash landing, enough was enough; she flaming well walked away leaving the pesky brat sucking on air! Her trouble was double with twins. By and by, the ewes would stalk over to Mojac and their union representative would gripe, "According to Webster's Suffolk dictionary, the word, wean, means get those butting bozos off our sore faucets like — toot of the sweet!"

Lambs, like children, grow incredibly fast. One minute they are wobbling and nursing; the next minute, there they are joyfully jumping over, on, up, and off hay bales. Five minutes later, or so it seemed, they were creep trained and growing fat on COB and alfalfa. Before we could blink, Mojac's babies were heading away from home.

MOVE YOUR
RAM BUTT

Taking lambs to market was an experience we learned to hate. The sheep were frightened, easily confused and hard to pen, and the handlers' approach toward the animals, needlessly cruel. Booted kicks substituted for gentle persuasion ninety percent of the time, prompting a lot of yelling — "Knock it off!" — from me. I misdoubt there is a lock on reincarnation but, if perchance, Mojac hopes some of those louts come back as sheep. Let me be fortunate enough to greet them — I guarantee a kick a day and nice fresh hay!

The market locale was a livestock auction, where if you reached up to scratch your itchy nose, you'll probably discover the last bid on a three-legged horse had just been made by ... who, me?

The auctions used a painful method to indicate the way livestock would be identified for ticketing in yon bidding ring. An ear punch, something like a one-hole paper popper, was used to attach a plastic tag to the animal's ear. Sheep have numerous small veins in each ear; but no concern or care was ever exercised. Bleeding veins, in some cases bleeding heavily, were not uncommon — not to mention the shock and pain experienced by your animals. Handling of lambs was not quite as mean or rough, but they were every bit as bewildered and frightened. The auctioneer had to identify ticketed stock in order to pay the seller and to make sure the buyer received the animals he bid upon and purchased; nevertheless, there are easier more humane ways to do it.

All farmers have to be able to identify and sometimes prove which animals belong to him, especially the ones that are registered. Thanks to The Shepherd magazine, Mojac had long since stopped punching big holes in the ears of our sheep. Instead, we used a tattooing machine much like that utilized on race horses. Traumatic and painful it was not. Like all sheep, ours were also determined to prove the grass was greener on the other side, thus, never again did we have to worry over shredded sheep ears caused by tags snagging on woven wire fencing.

Our auction woes continued when our animals, including our registered stock, failed to bring the prices they were worth. Prevalent thinking at stock auctions seemed to be that the rancher was dumping old, worn-out or sterile animals. I am sure that suspicion was sometimes justified, but not always. Culling to keep the herd strong often selected out good sheep. If your special ones did not sell privately, and they were not market wethers, then the despised auction became the last resort. Unfortunately, from time to time, Mojac had to bid good-bye to some of their top animals at those detested sales.

Herself was elected to guard the truck on all those miserable journeys. Personally, I would rather have taken Meg inside with us and let somebody steal the gas guzzler, but Mollie-O always reminded me of the long, long walk home, and Megan inevitably took on sentry duty.

Conversation in the truck remained subdued when Mojac headed home after one of those most depressing of days. Megan, aware that some of her old and young friends were missing, would lay her chin first on Mollie-O's leg and then on mine, canine commiserating with us both. The three of us truly loathed those livestock auctions.

-»>   «-

Mojac Farm's female party taught art. Art teachers instruct in many creative and challenging fields: watercolors, drawing, painting, weaving, posters, sculpting, clay and collage, to name but a few. One of her assignments led directly to Sheba sauntering through our front gate. Black yarn was needed for an arts and crafts project called, "Weavings." Sheba was a gorgeous black ewe. Soon, the wool of Mojac Farm's current addition became a great hit with Mollie-O's students and ensured many creative weavings. Notice how one thing leads to another on a sheep farm?

Our black momma was obnoxiously independent. Actually, she was downright antisocial, not only to us, but also to all the members of her sheep clan. Naturally, when Big Daddy strolled the neighborhood she cozied up to him. But, when Pop's interests tiptoed him away to different pastures, she once again ignored social niceties and bawled, "Buzz off," to any who offered friendship. Content in withdrawal, she parked her indifferent self in a far corner of the pasture. Her solitude wouldn't be broken until it became time to deliver her lamb.

Though fully grown, Sheba was nonetheless a small ewe who approached her deliveries like natal emergencies. Yes, she was independent, reserved and a solo act, but when our recluse's time to deliver became imminent, no. When the maternity angel whispered that soft message in her ear, Sheba would waddle over, statue in front of us, and glare her own impending birth message.

"Well, guys, the big moment's arrived. Are you two going to help me or not? Surely, you don't expect royalty to handle matters themselves?"

Responding to that desperate 911 call, Mojac's prompt services having quickly been rendered, Sheba soon presented us with a superbly handsome black ram. We named him — Ebon.

Sheba, maternal cares in hand and lamb in tow, promptly trekked back to her isolated pad of pasture. Ebon enjoyed playing with the other lambs, but never for very long. Soon a sharp blat would pierce the air: "Junior, haul your dusky frame back here on the double-quick!" Obediently and swiftly, the young Othello set sail in the direction of she whose commands will be obeyed.

Megan, herself sporting an abundance of black fur, approved of black sheep. Ebon was a kindred soul and she delighted in him. Nevertheless, when he was fully grown, he became the big, strong, silent type and Megan handled him with caution. Matter of fact I, too, trod lightly around him. Not out of fear, mind, for 'tis widely known I have the heart of a lion. Unfortunately, my feet are pathetic cowards and ... *I run with my feet!*

→≫   ≪←

Although Peppy wasn't getting any younger, running still related as joyful for him as for Megan. He could still pick 'em up and lay 'em down. Passersby in pickups — their dogs riding shotgun in back — often motored by, heading either out or in to the higher hills. When one or more dogs pass another member of the clan, everybody just naturally has to mouth off. Frequently, the insults get close and personal. On one such occasion, a couple of curs made disparaging remarks to Peppy as they rolled past in the bed of their pickup. Pep, inside the fence, insulted, swore back and kept pace with the truck.

More bad language was forthcoming from the truck's canines as the vehicle increased speed. Peppy likewise sped up and hurled a final epithet when the driver up-shifted and the pickup scooted away over the crest of the hill, like a bat out of ... ! Moving like the proverbial cat with its tail on fire, Peppy quickly Federal Expressed all the remaining swear words he knew and continued his valiant pursuit until Mojac's highway cross fencing brought him up short. Another not at all civil word for the road travelers and he panted his way back to flop on the front porch, there to lie in wait for the next loose-mouthed mongrel. Inevitably, on one of those roaring gallops, he was bound to injure some part of his long, lanky body. In this case, the pads on all four feet were bruised, torn and in need of some major TLC.

Continuing the tale, I must relate a bit more to you regarding his brief flirtation with high fashion. After cleaning, disinfecting and bandaging him, we pondered how to protect, and then insure, our galumphing goof would keep his paw-protecting coverings on when he walked. Mollie-O and David put their heads together (not necessarily an improvement) and up with the solution they came.

Residing in my bureau drawer, waiting patiently to return to fashion, were several long, mismatched argyle socks: One red, one blue, one with green diamonds, and one candy-striped. Calf length, for the impeccably styled and well dressed, these Van Gogh's in wool, soon slipped over Peppy's ouching feet, were hauled up to his shoulders and haunches, then held in place by suspenders that stretched over his back.

Presenting his one permanently floppy ear, his goofy expression and those ridiculous old socks, the duded-up bon vivant never looked so natty; his appearance harlequined that funny, we all totally cracked up! Megan was reduced to bouncing up and down, hiccuping and braying like a Grand Canyon mule. Dave and Mollie laughed so hard they cried. I remained quite staid except that, owing to a hurting belly, I couldn't stand up. Squeaky, the cat, stalked indignantly off to the barn, such loud guffawing having disturbed his afternoon siesta. Poor Peppy, he portrayed exactly a tail wagging Mortimer Snerd responding to Edgar Bergen.

"Duh, what's so durn funny — fellers?" Away we all whooped again.

THE BON VIVANT

Mollie-O

10

Meg Hears of Will'um

*Rams when circling about, the wise are prudent and ...
butt out!*

Mojac

"It will only be a ten minute job," Dave stated casually, as I
wearily unlimbered my sagging frame and fell out of the car after
another frustrating day trying to persuade young minds of the
importance of academic subjects, other than their choice of lunch
and recess. A gate needed repair, a light socket needed re-wiring,
the water heater needed new coils, the hay grinder needed attention,
a fence needed this, the barn needed that — need, need, need!

"It will only be a ten minute job, piece of cake." Ha! Every
one of those TMJs ended up grabbing from four to six hours and
prompted daydreams of a two week vacation at a five star resort
where, the only place lamb showed up would be on the menu;
whereupon, the cook's demise would be instant! Davey lad, sure
and I'm lovin' you like a brother, but sometimes I think you froze
more than your toes, mushing through snow in your sandals.

-≫>   ≪≪-

Mojac experienced a bizarre and sad happening with one of our pedigreed ewes one year. Maternally graced, she was a strong, prime Suffolk, a favorite of Meg's and a raiser of proud, robust lambs. Gradually, for no reason we could determine, mother ewe began to wane. Her illness developed slowly but progressed steadily, and the miserable malady defied diagnosis. As the debility advanced, our ewe also lost vision and lacked energy; sightless and listless, she continued to eat and did not lose weight, though her pleasure in life was gone.

The veterinarian speculated that a bug might have invaded a nostril while the ewe grazed and from there had begun a slow advancement upward into her brain which could account for her lassitude and loss of sight. Sadly, within a further week our unfortunate mother had to be put down. Autopsies expensive, money tight, Mojac was never to know the cause. Ewes, other than their own lambs, do not look after their own kind. Without guidance she could not find her way about the farm. Unable to see Megan, she could not obey her.

Dave kindly offered to put down and bury the ewe while we were away at school. Megan had already begun to mourn. Yes, Borders will grieve for a missing sheep, especially if the flock is small and each animal is known.

When brother David undertakes to perform his tasks they will be performed correctly, even ten minute whizzers! Accordingly, pick and shovel in hand, he chose the burial location carefully and proceeded to dig his way down to the valley floor! Not content with a random excavation, he decided to measure the precise dimensions of the grave.

How would you decide if a hole in the ground was wide enough, long enough and deep enough? If you were Dave, You'd have lowered your lanky six-foot two-inch frame into the pit and, lying down, stretch out for size. Flat on your back, gazing heavenward, you would then have observed five quite large and curious heads staring down at you. Although those faces are encircling your temporary abode, blocking the sun, what's to worry? They are sheep.

FIVE
BUDDIES?

Sheep are friendly — especially Mojac ewes.

That's strange, this group seems to be somewhat larger in size. In fact, they don't even have the same shape as female woollies.

Mother me darlin', flowers now on my grave you should strews, 'cause what I'm lookin' at surely ain't ewes!

Well, that sudden discovery made Big Dave nervous as a one-eyed sidewinder trapped in a Saturday night dancehall full of loggers. He bailed out of the pit — FAST. Scrambled across the pasture — FASTER. Cleared the closed gate — FLYING. His Marine Corps training had not prepared him for retreat, but what he lacked in experience, he made up for in SPEED!

Once his heart and nerves settled down, after an hour or two, Davey, walking very softly, oozed up to the ram pasture gate and quietly locked Big Beau and his four pals safely away from a private funeral. Now of course that's how David handled that particular job. I don't know what I'd have done. What about you?

Losing our prize ewe listed tragic, but hearing about Davey's ram adventure definitely eased the pain. That which remains unsure leaves an empty space, but it also makes room for the cricket on the hearth to chirp hope into our ears.

⇒⟫   ⟪⇐

A working animal farm comes with a variety of built-in chores. Some of these I called the nasties. Of those nasties, the nastiest was cleaning out the barn. It will e'er remain my favorite! Freshening was accomplished the old-fashioned "scientific" way: with a hand-held pitchfork; a bent back; a grunt, a heave and a plop into Chumley, the manure spreader. Crank up dear old Alfred, trundle away from barn to pasture, spread the phewey-phewey — remembering to duck or wear a hard hat — and then rattle directly back to the barn to fork up another loathsome load. Round trip after interminable round trip. Between sheep and cattle barns, "freshening" was a hot, stinking, backbreaking, full, four day job.

Megan, when she wasn't off bugging the ducks or checking on Beau, Old Blue and Gutface, would repose on a hay bale and supervise. Periodically a bark would issue forth from the throne. I always likened that to mean, "Guy, it smells really bad in here!" Huh, Megan should complain, after every bath who could hardly wait to roll herself around in the nearest pile? Unhappily, she was correct. Sheep manure is sniffingly pungent. After four spreader loads the odor wafting throughout the barn and up cringing noses was definitely not eau de Cologne.

In my hour of greatest need, a three-hundred-thousand-mile beater wheezed into the driveway and an older gentleman stepped out. After introductions, he informed me that, while he worked a small farm higher up on the Hill, he was barely making ends meet on Social Security. As he grew all his own produce he asked if he could be of service helping to clean out Mojac barns in exchange for several truckloads of sheep fertilizer. A botanical expert, among other things, for many, many moons, he highly prized sheep droppings and relished relating the value of their chemical contents. All I wanted was to see the last pile of phewey-phewey disappear and I recognized an answer to prayer when I saw one. I couldn't wait to shake hands on the deal!

Directly, his Datsun pickup converted into a side-racked flatbed, crowhopped backward into the barn and soon departed with loads of aromatic fertilizer.

Proudly claiming Indian ancestry he was also, as it turned out, an absolute fund of wonderful stories, many of which helped fill in the spaces between forking, grunting, groaning, cussing and — straining the springs on his Datsun!

On one particularly pungent phewey-phewey day, Megan and I memorized one of our Indian helper's best stories. I cannot swear to the facts, of course, because I wasn't there, but I can attest that what you are about to read has been faithfully recounted from the old timer's original version. Any good Oregon history book should make verification easy and you may want to look it up. You'll no doubt notice that one of my friend's most enjoyable talents was how easily he could slip into the vernacular of the times when yarning. Here is his sworn version of a touch of Oregon history.

How the Willamette River Was Named

by J. L. SMITH (furtrapper)

"Some years ago, back in the early thirties, my father took our family camping in the high Cascades. Three days into our hike we chanced upon an ancient log cabin sitting back among a grove of tall pines. Out front, a very old man with a noticeable limp was busily hoeing a row of raccoon pilfered corn and we exchanged greetings. He introduced himself as Justa L. Smith and invited us to camp there for the night, if we took to the notion. Our host informed us that he was one of the last of the old-time Mountain Men in Oregon. The "locals" and old time pards called him Justa Leaner Smith, because in his youth he had taken refuge in a cave from a dad-burned off-season snow storm. Happened a momma bear and two cubs joined him for company. By the time she had chewed off half his foot, he'd figured out four was a crowd and lit out for an unclaimed snowbank! He's been leanin' to the left ever since, which explains why — when he bothers to vote — he votes demycrat."

"A small creek drifted sleepily by the cabin, talking and chuckling to itself. In the early evening's quiet I could still hear it whispering. My father, a city man, conveyed his envy to the old trapper. Smiling, he agreed it was honest company — but just like all dad-blamed streams — it was downright garrulous and full of folk stories. by the way, would we like to hear one of them? "You bet," we shouted. Justa sat back, lit his pipe, cleared his throat — and began:"

Back uh spell they wuz uh heap a folks livin' in the East ez decided tuh uproot an' hit out fer a place called Orygun. This here story is 'bout one of them fam'ly's; leastwise, one member in particlar."

"This fam'ly, name a Sawyer, wuz a party a four. Ma, Pa, li'l sister, Rachel, an' a older boy name a Tom."

"The West wuz still young then an' yuh couldn't nowise scrag a rattler an' rail it thar, seein' as they wuzn't no rattlers tuh scrag! Most folks jes' choosed the 'scursion special an' chawed the dust by way uh horse an' wagon."

"Thet spring thuh Sawyers' 'lected tuh hitch on to a wagon train a'snakin' outa St. Looey, led by a old crowbait by way of Pizin Gut Pomfrey. Called such 'cuz of his habit uh drinkin' anythin' liquid in a sorta perm'nint challenge to his stomach! Howsomever, on accounta his breath ez mean enough tuh melt a glacier, he ain't never been froze in, an trail folk set a heap uh store by him."

"Directly, Pizin, the train, an' the Sawyers rolled outa St. Looey a-singin' a travelin' song — somepin 'bout doo-dah — an' everythin' woulda been jake 'ceptin' fer Thomas. In a prime effert ta contribute roundin' tuh yore edication this here is where I antes up a pitchur a Tom: First off, he wuz a boy ez wuz inclined tuh engage in certain harmless kinds uh escapades. Like thet time, jest fore dinner, he up an' dropped his pet frog in the fam'ly stew. Right soon, Ma hollered, 'Them ez comes, gits,' an', all unawares, poured Pa's plate full a frog. Fore a lick uh grace could be spoke thet critter hed jumped half-way down Pa's throat!"

"Then they wuz the time he nailed his sister's pantaloons to the privy door. She bein' in them at thuh time kinda drew Ma and Pa's attention tuh some peculiarities in Tom's way o' behavin'."

"Nother time he ... well, yuh got the big pitchur now. He weren't noways bad, jist a energetic, all aroun', fun-lovin' boy. Now how come yore so proud he ain't yores?"

"Pa, in a effort to keep Tom occupied along o' thuh trail, wuz plannin' on sendin' him off tuh play with the injuns; but they wuzn't no way thet'd work. Seems like Tom, while he were waitin' tuh dust outa St. Looey, engaged in sum little tradin' deals. a prize passel uh redskins, lodged on the edge of town, hed run intuh him. Seems like one deal were 'bout paintin' uh wigwam or a corral. Mebbe it were a horse or a fence. It were somethin' like that. Anyhow, them injuns hed done already clumb a high hill an' sent up the smoke on Tom! Soon's all their prairie brothers spotted thet kid a-comin', they done cayused intuh the nearest Elk's Lodge an' obliged they wuzn't comin' out agin till — winter!"

"Pa frazzled his head a hole lot about what to do with Tom. Then one day, most a third uh the way 'tween here and thar, a idear come. He jaws, 'Ma, I been studyin' a hole lot 'bout how we kin keep Tom happy an' otherwise engaged in a likely occupashun, ez I kin still taste thet frog. I b'lieve I finally thunk her out. Soon's thuh train gits dustin' intuh Independence we air a-goin' tuh git him a pet an' Tom kin take keer of it all by hisself. The critter will grow ez we roll, an' when we gits tuh Orygun we done got us a start fer stock.' Ma chortled, 'Pa, yuh shore air thuh smart one,' an' she peeled back her upper lip an' laid uh smack on Pa as boded her an interestin' time in Independence, too!"

"By an' by the big city hove intuh view. Thuh train soon squalled down Main street an' on thru tuh set up camp on thuh far side uh town where they wuz shade an' water. Quick's the Sawyers wuz settled, Pa an' Tom a-hoofed intuh thuh big booger tuh look fer the new pet. Late evenin' sun were a-smackin' Ma 'tween the eyes when they come moseyin' back."

"Tom hed his arms full o' pet an' a grin on his kisser big 'nough tuh walk on. 'Looky here whut I got Ma,' he hollers, 'His name ez a-goin' tuh be Will'um', an' Ah'm purely proud tuh be charged with takin' keer uh him; ain't he ever so genuwine han'some?'"

"A pig he were, han'some he plumb weren't! Howsomever, Tom were now reasonable an' he were-a-grinnin'. Rachel could visit the camp privy in peace an' she were-a-grinnin'. Pizin Gut Pomfrey knew where they wuz hid a batch uh aged, hunner'd proof, corn-squeezin's alkeehall, an' he were-a-grinnin'. Them injuns, way back in the lodge, were likewise-a-grinnin'; it were a brother as had traded Will'um tuh Tom. Pa wuz remembrin' Ma's smack back on thuh trail an' he were-a-grinnin'. Ma were remembrin' whut Pa were remembrin', an' she were-a-grinnin', too! (Thuh sun sets here, which jest 'bout takes keer of all thet remembrin')."

"Travelin' life smoothed considerable fair after Tom latched onter his Will'um. Nothin' much excitin' happened fer uh spell, so I 'spect this here's ez good a time ez any tuh fillyuh in on Will'um: which purely is a unfortunate choice o' words, 'cuz, fillin' in he weren't, fillin' out he were. Come vittle stuffin' times yuh dasn't say, 'Come an' git it,' aroun' Will'um. He'd git a look on his face so plumb joyous it wuz a pure crime tuh dassapoint him. Takin' a brief spell 'tween forkin' an' chawin' tuh lap rest yore hand were also a mistake. Fore yuh ever hit thuh mark, Will'um 'ud have yore hand an' be a-workin' on yore elbow! He jist weren't no ord'nary critter. In fact — whut Will'um were — he were a pig absoluterly determined to make a elephunk outa hisself!"

"Fer a long time now, things got so blamed peaceable thuh buff'ler wuz even thinkin' 'bout comin' back. Day after day, outer Independence, 'twere pick 'em up an' put 'em down, chaw dust, spit, pick 'em up an' put 'em down; 'Come an' git it.' Nothin' excitin' a-tall. Oh, they wuz thuh time Ma come a bustin' outa the brush hollerin' fer Pa, her skirts up aroun' her foredeck an' her pantaloons at halfmast on accounta — while tendin' tuh the day's necessaries — a big rattler give her fierce warnin'. Ma figgered he had some cheek! An' I near forgot, the Groggins' boy, Doofus, played, 'Bet a ol' wagon wheel cain't cotch a ol' toe.' Thet wagon, enjoyin' thuh game, obliged an' flattened ever one on his left foot. It weren't all bad tho, everbody called him Duckfoot after that which air shorely better'n Doofus! Naw, it were so blamed borin', Will'um wuz the onliest one enjoyin' the trail. Busy eatin' hisself inta elephunk size, he even come back fer seconds on — dust."

"One turrible tryin' day, though, everythin' changed fer thuh Sawyers. Will'um — suddenlike — done quit eatin'! Now that weren't altogether bad, ez he were already bigger'n a full growed buff'lo 'thout his hair. Tom jest figgered Fat Willy had a Injun Summer bellyache an' grits fer him would be twict as much come he burped it outen hisself. Onliest thing wuz, Will'um weren't no better next day, nor in uh week! Why would thuh lardy one — totally dedicated tuh increasin' his size three-fold an' ten — stop stuffin' his gut? Pa an' Tom, then Ma an' even teeny Rachel drug everythin' they could think of past his nose in a effert tuh tempt him tuh grind his molars agin. They tried lard an' bean leanin's, sweet tater pie, rabbit stew an' injun tea; no soap! Next come dried apple cobbler, Will's favorite, (Megan drooled here) chili an' beans, po' johnnycake, molasses flapjacks, stewed apreecots an' hasty puddin'; nothin' stirrin'! List'ners all I am here tuh tell yuh flat out, Will'um O' Grunt jest were not of a mind tuh tuck in an' trough empty nothin'!"

"After 'bout 'nother twenty-three days uh pickin' 'em up an' puttin' 'em down, most uh the hard trailin' were over. Orygun were reached, leastways thuh high country part, an' thuh train stopped tuh rest stock a spell. Ol' Pizin hadn't tooken his settlers thuh reg'lar way down the Gorge an' 'long the Columbia River. In his own words, 'Them other travelin' folks done took all thuh good land to thuh north. I aim's tuh head yuh all a tad further south where they's still plumb purty pickin's.' Well now, Pizin Gut seen the trail folk were plumb tuckered too, an' likewise needin' a rest fore startin' tuh tackle thuh hard trek thro thuh pass down intuh the big valley, so, Pizin circled thuh wagons on a high plateau right next tuh a sudden step gorge — west of an' 'tween Opal an' Timpanogus lakes. Pa hobbled their horses back a-ways from thuh wagons, in where the grass wuz tall, prime an' fillin'. B'low the bluff wuz thuh smell, sight, taste an' wet uh've a right sweet lookin' li'l stream a-bustin' tuh grow intuh a roarin' river."

"Tom, fearful worried 'bout Cast no Shadder Will'um, who, turrible puny, still weren't eatin', wuz off huntin', hopin' tuh slide squirrel pie over his pet's taste buds an' fotch him back ter the days uh piggy gorgin' an' grinnin'."

"Ma, busyin' herself with gettin' supper, weren't really concentratin'. She were fussin' 'bout Tom. He wuz frettin' so over Will'um's disinterest in gastronomic grit-gruntin' thet he wuz beginnin' tuh eye his sister's pantaloons agin. Ma knew thet wuz a bad sign. She also knowed thet if Tom's skin an' bones weakling shuffled off tuh Hog Heaven, they wuzn't 'nuff meat on him tuh qualify fer a skinny porkchop. Smellin' trouble nosin' aroun' thuh wagon like camp fever lookin' fer a stomach tuh knot, it's no wonder Ma — biscuit mixin" — reached up fer a ounce er two uh bakin' powder an' ladled back two dabs uh gunpowder 'stead. The one bein' housed right b'side of thuh other on thuh shelf. Her theory bein' thet if redskins come callin', suddenlike, knowin' they wuz allus hongry, she could whip 'em up a li'l shot uh Ma's puff pastry. Sort uh've a Friday Surprise yuh might say — they'd shore git a bang outa it!"

"Finished, Ma placed the lip smackers on a pan an' laid 'em in her camp oven fer tuh bake. Well, almost immediate one uh them give her notice an' she seen right away whut she'd done. Not inclined tuh reach their homestead afore Pa, Ma fetched them biscuits outen thuh oven right smart an' flanged 'em on the grass tuh cool."

"Happened those party snappers landed jest 'bout uh frog's ear downwind uh where Gaunt Will'um wuz reposin', a-dreamin' of thuh palmy days. Now, as hez been already tole he weren't eatin'; howsomever, thet noways meant he'd give up breathin'. Slim Willy give a sniff uh them biscuits an' opened one eye. Not havin' any serious designs on at thuh moment, he decided to try a couple. Unload the 'So long Will'um' rifle, Pa. I be a son-uh've-a-gun if'en he din't come outa thuh doldrums with a snort an' inhale a few more. Then — although 'tweren't a-tall proper — he belched loud 'nough tuh roll a peal uh thunder 'crost the door uh thet Elk's Lodge, uh long summer back, which decided them folk tuh cozy down indoors fer four or five more moons. After thet burp, a smile most beautific sashayed 'crost Will'um's snoot an' he up an' rapid swallered thuh rest uh Ma's belly busters. Hear now, one an' all, thet anorectic buff'lo wuz back amongst them what likes to eat, an' eat, an' — EAT!"

"Tom, totin' uh couple uh squirrels fer his pet, riz inta view 'bout then, a-comin' tuh check on 'Him-Who-Caint-Cast-No-Shadder'. An' when he seen the gorgin' an' gruntin' goin' on, he let out a yell powerful 'nuff tuh shake thuh Cascades. The young'un lit out runnin' 'cross the plateau, 'longside thuh gorge side, bellerin' fit tuh kill, 'WILL'UM ET, WILL'UM ET,' till the hole dang country were a-ringin' with 'WILL'UM ET!' (Megan jumped up and barked excitedly when she heard that.)

"O'course, most uh the folks on thuh train wuz doin' other things sides worryin' 'bout Will'um. Heck a mighty, how 'cited can yuh git 'bout a hog which ain't eatin'? Most uh've them

people wuz a-tendin' tuh needy camp chores an' enjoyin' the rest
Pizen Gut Pomfrey hed seen fit tuh allow. Two uh've 'em, a boy
an' his pap, wuz down by thuh river a-fishin' an' admirin' thet
vista uh peaceful purtiness. Thuh li'l feller, somewhat overcame
by Momma Nature's skill with paint' an' brush said, 'Pa, whut be
thuh name uh this here doozy talkin', bitty ol' river?'

"Well now, thet boy's pap weren't perfected with a rock hard
memory fer names, yet he lit up real quick with sudden under-
standin' when he heard Tom bellerin' up top thuh gorge.
Howsomever, yuh sure know how 'tis with travelin' words. By
thuh time they whipped a-crost thuh gorge, sneered at a passin'
eagle, wrestled with uh couple uh sky-spirin' pine trees, kissed a
few daisies, bounced ofen thuh far cliff an' then skidded back a-
crost thuh river, they wuz jest a mite tuckered, outa breath, an'
soundin' diff'runt. To the boy's pap, what Tom were yellin'
sounded a hole lot like, 'Will-am-ette.' So — ez thick sorghum do
— he oozes out thuh followin' tuh his Ma's pride, 'Why, thet thar
ez the Willamette — dammit! I hope tuh shout an' smile a lot
thet's a purty li'l chunk, or I shorely be's a sad-eyed mule, uh've
the Willamette River.'"

"Now it natur'ly follers thet durin' thuh evenin's do-se-do an'
sashay round, thuh boy's pap slipped the name uh the river tuh a
neighbor. Thet neighbor tole his neighbor an', fore thuh hole crowd
chawed dust agin a-clawin' down the pass, the name, Willamette
River, wuz ez fixed in their minds ez the taste o' Ma's biscuits wuz
in Will'um's. Meetin' other folks along o' thuh trail they up an' tole
them, too. An' thet ladies an' gentlemen, boys an' girls, all gentle-
folk an' sech is how the Willamette River done got its name!"

"Too bad 'bout Will'um tho. He got tuh feelin' thet perky an'
eatin' so well on Ma's allus in demand belly busters thet he grew
turrible top heavy. One day a-headin' through thuh pass towards
Eugene, he heavied intuh a turn — leaned too fur out — an'
brodied off inta Long Way Down Gorge. (Meg, covering her eyes
with her paws, whined when she heard this sad news.)

"Willy hez latched onta his place in history tho. They done
named a river after him, an' then a big valley, an' I be dogged
if'en they din't go an' name a university honorin' his name, too!
The Sawyers — bein' respectful tuh his memory — built a nice

little trail stop at thuh very spot whar he porked out. They call's it Will'um's Do-Drop-Inn. Yuh all should et thar. Thuh specialty uh've thuh house ez still three large pork chops an' biscuits fer thirty cents."

"Say, pards, heve yuh ever heard how Champoeg (rhymes with phooey) done got its name?"

WILL'UM
ET

With the presentation of historical facts like that, it wasn't long before the barn was fresh and clean again for another season. Mojac's arrangement with their entertaining friend continued throughout the rest of our stock raising years.

11

Meg and Silver Creek Falls

Behold: Trees growing with abandon take the uninhibited view.

Mojac

My tale-telling friend was a man who, with trouble beating on the door, offered his help first. In the span of time I knew him, he never lacked for knowledge nor was he ever at a loss for effecting repairs. Quite elderly himself, he delighted in relating tales of his mother, who was still living. Those stories, including the one you just read, were always interesting, amusing and colorful. Megan and I doted on them and couldn't wait to hear the next one. Some few further years down the road myself now, I remain most grateful to him.

In relating a story of another pursuit as apiarist, the old boy slyly honey-tongued a message for avoidance of sting. He advised me to stand quietly before the hive — prepare like one of the Old Ones — and chant:

"Honeybee, honeybee, why must you sting?
When gathering sweet nectar, the tiny birds sing.

Sting me but once, 'cuz you angry, 'cuz you mean,
An, I gonna open yo hive an' pop yo queen!"
"How would your ancestor prepare?" I asked.

"He'd put a dab of honey on his nose and stand in front of the hive with his hands behind his back!"

This Mojac chicken — from a position of pure cowardice — decided not to put his advice to the test! Good luck if you decide to gamble your hide!

In truth, I had always believed that my old friend was never stung because he smoked like a flaming chimney. Any bee trying to pop a stinger into him would perish of lung cancer long before it ever penetrated that carcinogenic skin!

As the years passed, his ancient Datsun puffed and struggled up the hill with countless full loads of Mojac manure. My partner absolutely swore by his "green fertilizer," which he brewed by forking phewey-phewey into a fifty gallon drum filled with water. Allowed to age for a short time, the resultant green liquid was pailed from the drum and lovingly ladled over his row crops. It worked a treat and his garden (somewhat odoriferous during feeding) became the neighborhood envy.

Drive by a milk cow dairy, there are many in our vicinity, and observe the effect of liquid cow manure, sprinkler-spread over grass, alfalfa or corn. The superb growth and quality is unbeliev-able. Of course, the slurry pond's effect on the surrounding neighbors is somewhat severe. Watch out! Between a permanent cramp to the hand from holding the nose, coupled with a fixed grimace on the face, driving can become hazardous. Unfortunately, a slurry pond is a forever stink; the solution, other than blowing it up, is to move to the next county.

When I dispersed chunk phewey-phewey over the Mojac fields it was the twenty-four hour, aromatic, nose twitching kind and nobody hated me, I hope!

⇒≫ ≪⇐

Mollie-O, Megan and I were struggling with weeds one afternoon, attempting to prepare the garden for planting. I was wrestling with Cecil, my ancient shoulder-separating rototiller, when a young man on a modern tractor pulled up on the road. Eyeing the situation, he asked if we would like that little bitty piece of ground tilled with his machine? Having already nearly mulched Megan's tail with my herky-jerky bone buster, I was only too ready to accept his friendly offer. Before you could flip a flapjack our weed infested garden was freshly ground to a fine powder, quite ready for seeding. His pay? One glass of orange juice. Why the hip-hip hooray? Maybe what he did was no big deal, but it was a generous kindness.

We were pleased to become acquainted with the folks across the road from Mojac Farm. They had started a Christmas tree farm from scratch and then steadily developed a thriving business raising nursery stock. Like two beavers trying to outrace the coming of a long, hard winter, they wore themselves to a frazzle, slaving from burning daylight into soft, glowing dusk. Growing their evergreens, from seedlings to those under which Santa placed his packages for good little boys and girls, did occupy most of their time. But regardless of their own pursuits, those two never hesitated to offer help when needed.

Prior to the installation of our electric fence, Mollie-O and I would frequently chug home from school to find that the Mojac jumping cattle, off roadway exploring again, had been rounded up and were safely re-pastured. An added bonus — lawsuits weren't impending!

Arriving home another day, Mollie-O was informed of the possibility one of Mojac's lambs had taken it on the lam. Checking the highway, she soon spied the little twit happily joggy trot-trotting down the road heading for Adventureland. She tossed him into the station wagon and trundled him home to Mom. Through similar and countless escapades, nothing was too much trouble for our watchful neighbors across the road.

A LAMB ON THE LAM

Mollie-O

One summer, to reduce our winter feed costs, I purchased ten tons of u-load hay from a valley farmer. His many-acred farm lay some thirty miles away. Discovering Mojac's need for a bigger truck, our tree farm neighbor offered the use of his flatbed. I had never driven such a huge beast so he also volunteered to drive, instruct me in the art of shifting its gears, and help load. The big flatbed allowed us to transport the entire ten tons in only two trips, but my friend's work would go begging in the meantime.

Nevertheless, when we returned late to Mojac after a long hot day of loading the hay bales, he offered to stay to help me unload and store them in our sheep barn loft. I declined his offer (having already imposed enough on his kindness) and sent him home with my heartfelt thanks, after accepting his further offer of the truck for Mojac's personal use on the morrow. Money, as usual, preferring to reside in some other soul's bank account, Mollie-O and I couldn't scrape up two spare farthings to pay for his time, he wouldn't have taken them anyway!

After chowing down, Mollie, Megan and I hoisted, stacked and stored bales until we moved like zombies. Megan mostly supervised, making sure the two hundred bales were placed in neat, orderly rows. You'd think such heady work would drastically shorten her longevity!

Early the next day, we trekked back to the valley for the balance of our load. I handled the truck like a pro. Okay, once in a *long* while, Mollie-O asked me to grind her a pound, too. Smart aleck!

Loading was accomplished using a portable wheeled chute that fastened to the truck's side. This chute, facing forward and sloping upward from the ground, had a flared mouth. As the truck traversed the rows, the catcher's mouth captured bundles individually and sent them aloft to the truck bed. Standing on the flatbed, a lucky snagger grabbed the arriving bales and laid them across the bed, one layer at a time, east to west. The next layer was stacked north to south to lock in the layer below. Procedure then reverted east to west for the third course, and each succeeding level continued in the same manner until the load either crippled the truck or killed the stacker. After Mollie-O tossed the coin (I know she used a two-headed peso), I became the unfortunate snagger.

While I slogged, Miss Megan counted the rows and reminded me to securely rope the bales. Contending with two females at once is too much to ask of any male!

LOAD THAT BALE

About the time I knew I couldn't toss another bale, we were heavied out and rolling. Arriving at Mojac still loaded, (which, considering the still to do slugging, wasn't a bad idea) we performed the zombie routine again. This time, Megan kept her mouth shut!

Once all the bales were safely stored in the loft, I swept the hay debris away, off and out of the truck and then filled the tank with gas. (Our farm had its own pump.) Meanwhile, Mollie-O packed a box with her preserves and picked a large bouquet of flowers from the garden, which we delivered along with the truck to our friends. They are truly special people and Mollie-O and I have often wished we'd been able to adequately express our gratitude.

I include these brief stories to counteract the daily litany of misery reported on television and in the newspapers. Visit a newsroom. Perusing articles such as: a young lad gave up lunches for a month in order to help a pal learn his times tables or, a man travels two miles every day in his wheelchair to carry his own, garden grown, flowers to shut-ins in a rest home, etc., and the reporters all come down with big cases of the yawns. Let a blurb hit the wires about an anaconda swallowing a Volkswagen with a baby in it, and everybody springs to life. Why, they even let their coffee grow cold. Okay, I might have followed that one, too, but do you get my drift? Unfortunately, the media prosper when reporting the lowdown and dirty. Witness how they garner the big bucks by blatantly invading privacy and peddling trash. I believe that the media also have a responsibility to keep us informed about what the good guys are doing. Forget this nonsense that "nice guys finish last." Peddling news is a story business, and every life is a story, of good or evil. That's why I thought you should read about some of the good guys. Refreshing, wasn't it?

-»>   «<-

It was already mid September. Having reported back to school, we were again attempting to stimulate young minds. Blessedly, the pace on Mojac Farm always slowed a touch during late summer and early fall and most of the farm's requirements had been accomplished: a new crop of lambs, weaned and out to pasture; our hay had been cut, raked, baled and stored for the winter; another season of crummy market auction trips was behind us; the barns were clean and ready for a fresh supply of "cherry pits" (phewey-phewey); most of the garden vegetables were harvested; the woollies were shorn, dipped, tagged and their feet clipped; the ewes had been flushed and were dating Big Dad; we'd sold and delivered Mojac's wool; the food locker was lambed, porked and beefed; fall's raspberry crop was picked, frozen or preserved; the house and fences (including fifteen gates and wellhouse) painted and, wherever needed, repaired; Pep's fourteen and one-half acres of electric "ouch" fence inspected and tightened, waited eagerly to shock the unwary; our winter grain was housed in the big barn; and finally, all lamb scarper holes had been slammered. Surprise! Megan wasn't even tired! Ha! Mojac could even take time to enjoy pond and pets.

Yessir, Mollie-O and I could just plain relax. Who cares if winter's foul frigorific breath would soon freeze our necks! Did we give a rip? Did Meg?

Megan knew that right now the full-colored, eye-filling beauty of autumn leaves was waiting to enchant us at Silver Creek Falls. She decided that playing hooky at the falls listed at the head of her "goof off" agenda. "Amen to that." said Mojac. In no time, she had explored every immaculately kept bicycle, hiking and bridle path in the park, and she had memorized names and locations of the — always spectacular in winter and spring — series of falls, some of which continue to impress and remain a joy to the eyes during summer and into fall.

Undeniably, Oregon once displayed the finest system of highways, rest areas and state parks, in the nation. Shamefully, that fact is no longer true today, but not for lack of resources. Why then? With a population over three million, Oregon cruises third from the top in taxes levied. But big trucks pulling double and triple trailers beat the tar out of the Beaver state's roads and freeways. Studded tires cruelly thump the macadam, too. Also, we count our share of human skulkers — jackasses who train in vandalism. Oregon boasts more state government buildings per capita — most built within the last thirty-five years — than any of the stout monied states. Clearly — while busily lunching on the multitudes' bread — our political twits would rather build another grand edifice than preserve the ones that Ma Nature already installed. I can't figure it out but it surely cinches up the strangle knot on my Christmas necktie!

Flang it! Let's double time back to Silver Creek Falls. The Y. M. C. A. built a splendid camp there, where for some years our fifth and sixth graders participated in a three day Outdoor Education program. Pretend you are one of the participants. Here's a typical riddle to get you in the mood:

What hibernates all winter, snoozes in spring, cures hams all summer and, as payment in the fall, gets oiled? Dying for the answer? Search for the Missing Fence!

Big brag! Our school pioneered Outdoor Education in Salem and participated for many years. Two hundred kids had an absolute ball while seven teachers and the team leader (me), along with college and high school student aides, rode herd twenty-four hours a day for three days! Have you ever kept a bleary eye peeled in two hundred different directions for over four thousand three hundred and twenty long, long, l-o-n-g minutes?

As we planned for the experience to be both enjoyable and educational, our five-six team preferred scheduling quarters in late spring. Thus, our annual science instruction concentrated on botany, ecology, stream erosion, fish and wildlife, protection of environment, geology, weather, plant identification, social behavior in large groups (guess who picked that one?), and keeping flaming well quiet on the hiking trails so as to observe the deer ... before they stampeded!

Mudder Nature permitting, most lessons were conducted outdoors. Notebooks were required, observations had to be penned. Essays were also assigned and, we hoped, the curriculum chewed, swallowed and digested. Staff did not want nor allow two hundred students to become bored or, worse yet, lapse into mischief. Lettered on the other side of the page, the camp-out was also devised for enjoyment. There's no reason why some learning cannot be fun while at the same time remain serious business. By the same token, I don't hold with the theory that all learning should be fun — life ain't that way, brother!

Team students, who could afford it, paid their own way. To help others, the team's teachers devised a free enterprise system like you won't believe!

All year, bottles were collected and redeemed. I, putting on my Red Skelton act, clowned it up and conducted auctions (we sold everything but the baby brothers — I put the nix on that). Craft and bake sales during the school year and even during summer layoff also fattened the coffers. When every fund raising half-baker we could think of had been exhausted, we totaled up the take, subtracted it from the cost for camp and food, and divided the balance by the total number of paying students to calculate the individual cost. All students participated, regardless of their ability to pay. Sleeping bags and camping gear for those without were begged borrowed or purchased. To save money, we purchased our own grub, some cooking utensils and hired the cooks.

I rewarded our "mother's delights" by providing a duty roster: Waiting tables, KP (students bussed their own dirty dishes to the kitchen), cleaning tables and sweeping the lunchroom were a necessary part of the camp experience. Kids were responsible for the care of each group cabin, including bath and shower rooms.

Students, albeit reluctantly, did take showers! Cabins were inspected and a shiny quarter had better bounce off each bed! Not really, but I did check closely for the juvenile, "throw it in the funky closet or under the bed and Mother will never know," gambit. Teachers ate with the kids at each cafeteria table. Good manners were the rule!

At morning assemblies: the day's activities were outlined, assignments handed out, guest instructor specialists introduced, and head counts tendered to me by the aides (Woe betide those late to assembly!). Once their site locations were identified on students' maps, they were off to class and I began my endless routine of checking, checking, and checking!

State wildlife experts along with school specialists conducted most lectures. Staff and students were most impressed and grateful. Questions were fielded with consummate grace and never a put down (it's so easy to hurt the feelings of the young); our guest instructors were always willing to answer the same query over again. They treated our youngsters courteously and the wee scamps responded like young ladies and gentlemen.

When clutching twilight descended, a crackling, towering bonfire chased away the dusk, and we celebrated the day with music, singing, jokes and skits, which usually targeted team teachers. Mostly, our little darlin's nailed ... me! I wonder why? To begin the festivities, are you ready for an aide joke?

Three boyos, one English, one Irish and a wee Scot, all short of funds, wanted to view the Olympics. The Englishman, a quick thinker, shouldered a tree limb, hiked confidently to the entrance gate and said, "Bertram, Great Britain, pole vault." He was allowed to enter. Quickly, the canny Scotsman hefted a manhole cover, strode up to the gate and burred, "MacRoy, Scotland, discus." He, too, was granted entry. Not to be outdone, the Irishman, spying a loose roll of barbwire in a ditch, carefully hefted it, then toted it to the gate and brogued, "O'Judge, Ireland — fencin'."

Searching for promised camp drama, a veil of smoky mist tentacles into darkening woods. Campers sit arced before snarling, spitting flames, telling ghost stories (outrageous lies) along with gruesome tales, which lead the innocent into — skit time. With our aides help, the students have written these fearsome, blood-curdling acts. Herewith, the five-six team's all time favorite skit.

Bring in the dog. Lock and bar your doors. The following is not for the faint of heart, nor the squeamish:

HARK! Wolf howls sound from those deep, dark, closing woods. Kids aren't scared and yet, why do they edge closer together? Logs blaze and spark. A vague, grotesque figure, its upper torso totally hidden in a blanket because it is a a horribly ugly monster, is dragged forth from the darkness and forced to stand before the fire, facing spectators. Growls, moans and howls emanate from the unnatural creature. Two students choose a male victim from the audience and haul him — struggling fiercely to escape — in front of the ogre. Slowly the blanket is raised. The male sacrifice looks in horror — shrieks — faints!

A second captive, a kicking, screaming female, is forced in front of the beast. The blanket again is inched upwards. She stares — cries out — faints! Next, those two cruel escorts (whose names are recorded in my little black book) collar me. I do not fight. I am not afraid. I face the vile, hooded creature calmly. Ever so slowly the blanket ascends, up, up, and — horrors! — the monster emits a blood curdling scream — and faints! That one always totally cackled the audience.

Another skit used an aide impersonating me inspecting a cabin. Nervous students stood before their bunk beds. Question to a student, "How many warts on my toad?" Answer, "I dunno, sir." The aide hollers, "Your punishment, forty lashes with a wet noodle." Question to the second testee, "How many boils on a boiled egg?" Answer, "Dunno, sir." Impersonator screams, "Sixteen tadpoles down your back!" Question to next sufferer, "How many wrinkles has a prune?" Answer, "I dunno, sir, but if you'll smile I'll count them!" Audience knocks self out with laughter. I don't ever get no respect. After roasted marshmallows and that final nighty-night song, sleepy campers, sent off to bed, were treated to a sugar climax. Here I really lucked out, one of the team's male teachers had a sweet lip. He and I would pace quietly away to the camp flagpole and then, that darlin' lad would raise his horn and ever so sweetly — blow taps. Can a day ever end any better than that?

My memories of our Silver Creek Falls camp-outs are numerous, varied, happy, fresh and precious. Kids are so much fun. How blessed we all were.

Outdoor Education was an extensive undertaking. Our preparations began early in September and concluded in May. Because my colleagues were willing to go the extra mile and never overlooked a detail, our outings always fit in the successful slot. Although every year was physically and mentally draining, and they were never paid an extra dime for participating, the whole team volunteered year after year. Watching as the students joked and laughed, played, acted, sang, ate, dreamed (flat on their backs in lush meadows), worked, enjoyed, were mosquito bitten, scraped knees, noses and elbows, cemented lifelong friendships, saw teachers in a different light, and ... learned. Oh, yes, we were definitely paid.

Our sunburned little cherubs could hardly wait to go again. The team would heave a sigh and wheeze, "Why not? Isn't this what teaching is all about, dying in rapid stages while still ... young?" Tottering off to the team office, I would shakily pick up the phone and sign us up again for next year.

For seventy-two hours, primary responsibility was mine for the welfare, transporting, feeding, housing, and protecting, of two hundred children attending our Camp Outs each year, but make no mistake, the program never would have succeeded without the tireless contributions of my fellow teachers, classified staff, college and high school aides, and parents who volunteered to help.

Outdoor Ed took off in Salem, as school after school decided to participate. Our team had now chosen to rent a private camp off the North Fork of the Santiam River for our safaris. Quarters were a touch less rustic and completely enclosed. The elements could no longer close down and chase us home as had a really late deep freeze at the Y. M. C. A. camp one year, where the cabins were screened, but not enclosed. The logistics at that time, of packing, gathering, transporting and informing parents to pick up their frosty-nosed kids at the school — long after dark — don't bear remembering. I'll love our secretaries until the day I die for their heroic efforts in running down and matching each student to the correct family, that distressful trip. Amazingly, no one got lost and no one caught a cold.

Students were not stuck with K. P. at the new camp other than serving tables. We approved menus, the camp hosts and owners prepared and cooked the food. Dining service remained family style and tables continued to be hosted by the teachers. And of course, dirty-dish-bussing and cafeteria clean-up happily remained a joyful experience for the — children!

In the ten year span of Outdoor Education programs, during my tenure at the school, not one serious injury to student or adult was ever experienced; although, one of the youngsters, a young lady, suffered a badly sprained wrist and I thought it best to send her home. No way! She begged to be allowed to stay. As I happened to have two aces in the hole, I gave in.

Would you like to hear about my two aces? Husband and wife, they are doctors; coincidentally, I happened to be one of their children's teachers. Another of our Outdoor Education desires was to persuade qualified medical personnel to hie forth into the bush with us, always providing we'd managed to raise funds for the trip.

Our parent-doctors participated voluntarily for two years running. Would that entail sacrifice? Both physicians had to arrange for other doctors to handle their practices, to be reciprocated for at a later date. In addition, they provided their own transportation and paid all their own costs for the three days. Those two stayed with the team on call twenty-four hours a day. Between each meal, while teachers were instructing, what occupied the doctors' time? How about for all three days they took it upon themselves to clean, stack and feed the dishwasher. Later, one or the other remained at the side of my wounded bird dispensing TLC while the freed one was asking staff to be assigned wherever needed. Remuneration? Ha! Those two wonderful people would not accept one penny. Two aces, both of them with mighty big hearts!

One year, Mollie-O's peers awarded her the honor of Teacher of the Year, in recognition of her many accomplishments. I was unable to attend the banquet because I was in camp with my kids and they had to come first. I'm sure my wife was disappointed, yet she never complained. Mollie-O knew that, had the situation been reversed, her students would also have received top priority.

Mollie-O also led her school's third and fourth grade co-op team into Outdoor Education. Taking her responsibility truly to heart, she would not desert her kids even when she contracted pneumonia. Collapsing upon her return from camp, she used up all her sick leave recovering. Some months later, a school board member, in blanket assertion, roundly pontificated, "Teachers — having expended all their sick leave — deserve firing!" So much for Mrs. Mollie-O Judge, Salem's teacher of the year!

Dedication is and should be part of a teacher's code of ethics. Over a decade, two thousand kids attended our Camp Out Programs. Once, only, I had to send a student home for unacceptable behavior; and only once, regrettably, did I fire an aide. How extremely fortunate for me to have been allowed leadership over such a talented and professional group of dedicated teachers.

SILVER
CREEK
FALLS

12

Meg and the Missing Fence

Graduate 'A' of the dense when repairing the flaming fence!

Mojac

My thanks for permitting that small detour on the previous pages. Silver Creek Falls was important to Mojac from a professional as well as agricultural point of view. Besides, Megan and I hope your interest has been piqued and you will pen an addendum to your weekend visitations agenda. Stop off at the Falls — winter or summer — and set a spell. You'll not be disappointed.

≈≫ ≪≈

Answer to riddle: *A trail rider's saddle.* Ouch! So why are you turning nasty? Our kids thought it was a hoot. Grumpy Outdoor Education sneezers you'd be!

≈≫ ≪≈

Winter had been an Oregon buster. A whistling, wheezing walloper! Between black ice, snow, rain and silver thaws, it was colder than a bare bod wrapped around an iceberg. Mollie-O and I slipped all over the bleeding roads hying to and from our schools. Never was Spring Layoff looked forward to more. Accordingly, I bade my charges spend a safe, happy week and headed for the hills. It calendars March 16th, late for really bad weather here in Webfoot Land so — naturally — I drove smack into a snow storm! The Mo part of Mojac had the station wagon that day and slithered home about half an hour after me. By that time I'd had a litter of kittens and was working on a flurry of fowl.

Grateful that Mollie-O was still in one piece, I headed out to feed the stock. Surprise! Seven minutes later a little old lady who really should not have been out in all that slop, slid off the road and wiped out one hundred feet of our highway fence! Cars, regardless of the Indianapolis 500, were not meant to fly. Fortunately, although pretty well frazzled and trapped in her car, she suffered no serious injuries. Her car was resting at a severe angle, courtesy of the highway ditch, which had a decided drop at that section. Of course, that ditch had never stopped our wayward steers!

While awaiting the rescue vehicles, Molly wrapped the unfortunate old girl, as securely as the situation would allow, in one of our warmest blankets, and provided commiserating company until help arrived.

I have to say, those volunteer first aid and fire department people from the Hills were highly skilled and first rate. In one flick

THE
MISSING
FENCE

of Megan's ear, out came the shook-up driver and away off to her home she went where, I trust, a strong libation awaited, at least a double.

Meanwhile, snowbound and forlorn in Mojac's pasture, lay the dead car! Megan, Mollie-O and I, surrounded by nosy sheep, were left in a howling, snowy nor'wester staring blankly at a hundred feet of torn and flattened fence.

Megan and I herded the woollies into the safety of the barn. After feeding and watering the flock, and also tending the cattle, we mushed on up to the house, cheering the weather.

Next morning, I made a terrible mistake. I got out of bed. Goof number two: I decided to repair the damaged fence myself. Despite Mollie-O and Megan's wise counseling to the contrary, I remained firm in my resolve. To this day, I think my brain had definitely been frozen.

I wasn't worried about the cost. I knew our unexpected visitor's insurance company would be delighted to pay for the repairs. My concern was when would Mojac's beat up fence get fixed? This will surprise you, but sometimes repair people are possessed of minor peculiarities, like not showing up to do the work on the appointed day. Or, most obligingly having penciled an estimate, choosing a work date in the first place! "Yep, ah kin do thet little ol' job, easy. Howsomever, we cain't get to 'er this week. I has ta take thuh ol' lady an' our kids over tuh Eastern Orygun fer spring grouse huntin'." How about, "Nope, fishin' season be startin' in 'bout two weeks an' I done already got muh license. How's 'bout we whippies yore fence back intuh shape in May or June?" It's ever so much like a dentist a-pullin' yore teeth, it don't pain him none 'lessen he ain't paid! In the meantime, I had a pasture full of sheep who saw any breach in the fence — let alone one hundred feet of clear sailing — as an invitation to ramble.

Megan, Mollie-O and I spent that frigid, wet, miserable layoff week slipping, slogging, slithering, squishing and squalling! When not delivering lambs (ah yes, the ewes were delivering on schedule), we extracted broken posts and set new ones, removed ripped and torn wire and replaced it with new. We spent the rest of the time fetching needed materials (at least we were out of the muck for this one). Finally, Hapless Construction reinstalled the torn portions of the electric fence and then tested it. In between, Megan straw-bossed the wrecking crew while they tore up Mojac's pasture dragging that fender bent clunker back onto the highway. Repairs completed, I penciled up the tab while sipping a hot toddy in a desperate effort to ward off pneumonia: Some for the posts, some for the wire, some for staples, some for truck gas. I came up with a figure of $50.00 for materials, and I threw in the labor. Better believe I've got a head for sums!

It sure had been a fun week and I was already looking forward to summer layoff; when maybe the barn would collapse. I received a check from the insurance company by return mail. Included in the envelope was a notice to cash immediately. Now I wonder why they did that?

Regardless of that muddy, cold, wretched week, I was ever so grateful to another of the farm-inherited work savers. Second only to Alfred in importance, re mechanical equipment, the grand old fellow was our hauling trailer. The frame was a wooden, six by ten flatbed, the front, back, and sides rose but six inches and all those boards were removable. Best of all, the bed tilted. Muchas gracias, and an olé to the designer. The trailer tongue was a fourteen foot piece of pipe, six inches in diameter. A hitch capable of fitting the ball on Alfred had been welded to the front end. Truck wheels bearing tires, lugged onto a five hole standard axle, allowed for movement. A piece of steel with a three-quarter inch hole drilled in it had been welded to the top of that tongue at the point where the bed, returning from the tilt, lowered to sit. Two more pieces of metal, each having also had a three-quarter inch hole drilled in it, had been welded to the bottom of the bed so that they rested, one on each side of the one on the tongue. Those three holes, once aligned, allowed a steel rod to be inserted which locked the bed in place. Mojac named the trailer, Cuthbert.

Cuthbert volunteered to haul everything on the place, from hacked out blackberry vines to firewood; he toted creosote treated posts needed to support the farm's metal gates (the farm counted fifteen all told), which replaced the old wooden ones as soon as I could afford to buy them; the trailer carried bentonite (ten ton!), gravel, and our dead ram and ewe. Cuthbert had just hauled the items needed to effect repairs to the flattened fence: wire, tools, staples, posts and a come-along. Serving further, he toted Megan, who loved to ride on him whether he was laden or not. The trailer did seem to draw the line on hauling phewey-phewey and in a most gentlemanly way kindly referred me to the manure spreader. In short, Cuthbert was our master of all trades! I don't know what I'd have done without him.

⇒⟫ ⟪⇐

Although winter has a bad reputation, she isn't all rotten. True, she does bring the rain, but she also generously returned Mojac's winter creek. I can't think for the life of me why I haven't mentioned that creek and our wellhouse before now. I shall make up for that lapse immediately. The farm house situated on a knoll. Below, in a grove of alder trees in the main pasture, about one hundred and thirty yards away in a northwesterly direction, sat the wellhouse. Our winter creek, starting midway on the east boundary line and meandering completely through the property, ran to and under the highway on the southwest. Mojac's wellhouse had been constructed in the shape of a little cottage, complete with windowed door, and included a white fence all around to keep nosy sheep away. Inside, I always left a lamp lit. At night, the light, like a candle in the window, cheered and welcomed us home. In addition, it was always the last place I eye-checked before retiring of a night. Its glow reassured, much like an adult security blanket and, silly as it may sound, I took comfort from it. During the winters, I doubled the bulb's wattage and also placed another lamp directly over the pump so as to keep it from freezing. A one hundred watt bulb suspended over pump and pipe and then surrounded by cardboard sides definitely added to the cheer. A farm may do without many things, but water isn't one of them. Thawing frozen pipes in freezing weather does not tran- quilize the temper. Thanks to that soothing light, I continued to maintain the equanimity befitting the always benign. And if the bulb were to burn out? I would, sometimes in PJ's, robe and slippers, make it down to the wellhouse quicker than a skunk closing down a garden party!

A waterwheel had been erected in the creek to the left of the wellhouse. This old love, except for a steel spindle upon which she revolved, was built entirely of wood. Motion of her wheel's wooden paddles through flowing creek water, collecting and then gently returning, seemed like friendly conversation, which for me, equated stream and wheel with living things. Occasionally a stranger, winter sun, would turn the water droplets into prisms, then flash the colors of the spectrum at mole-blind eyes — a rare treat. Yes, it has to be said, winter does have her good side.

➣➣   ⫷⫷

On Sunday, May 18th, 1980, at 8:32:59 a.m., Mount St. Helens threw-up! She had been serving notice of her indigestion for weeks, constantly burping like a baby with a bad load of gas. Her misery must have been acute. I'd seen the result of that kind of inner turmoil only once before, aboard a merchant vessel, where a shipload of GI's foolishly dined on Cookie's, long-time-no-sea, fish stew!

Herewith a few facts, just enough to whet your appetite as there are some excellent books on the grand old dame, readily available for study in your local library:

When her tummy could no longer hold it, she tossed her cookies over fifty thousand feet into the atmosphere in one quarter of an hour. That translates into a height of almost fifteen miles in a span of fifteen minutes! The black cloud contained between 1.7 and 2.4 billion cubic yards of material. Talk about a potent stew. Because she spewed directly upward, a zone of silence covered a sixty mile radius, which explains why, on the fringes of that circumference, Mojac did not hear the lady's humongous burp! Inside the devastation zone, 4.7 billion board feet of Douglas fir, cedar and hemlock — leveled — looked for all the world like a gigantic pile of jackstraws laid out over eighty-six thousand acres. The terrible heat melted seventy percent of her snow which ran down the mountainside, triggering massive mud slides and floods. Harry Truman, the eighty-three year-old caretaker of Mount St. Helens' Lodge, who had visited school children in Salem the previous week and vowed not to leave his beloved Spirit Lake, perished under a three-hundred-foot avalanche of rock.

Outside the devastation zone, fourteen to seventeen miles away, St. Helens' breath was searing enough to kill trees but not strong enough to flatten them. That section is called the scorch zone. Airborne ash from the eruption reached Boston in two days and completely circled the globe in just seventeen!

Megan positively flew from the barn to the house, hurrying to blow the whistle on Big Momma Mountain. I've never been able to figure how animals know when Mother Nature is flipping her lid; or, in that case, that the old bag already had, yet they always do.

Mojac didn't see the big bang! Flying with the crows, our farm is about sixty-five miles away. Although we could and did see the cloud of ash at altitude and felt a slight rumble, we were denied actual sight of her bla-hooey because higher hills above us blocked the view.

Fortune smiled on most Oregonians that day. The jet stream carried the bulk of St. Helens' ash cloud to the north and east. Yakima, Washington, about the same distance east of the mountain as Mojac Farm is south, was hard hit. We received but a light sprinkling of residue, which, if anything, fertilized pastures.

A thin layer, about one-third of an inch, took up residence in the farm's eave troughs. In my usual brilliant fashion, I made haste to rid me of the gray gunk before drains became plugged. Had I been thinking, I could have gathered up that historic dust, divvied it with Mollie-O, and we could have taken it to our schools for the kids to mix with clay, then create and kiln fire some St. Helens' artifacts. My flaming school would have become famous, renowned the world over for its contribution to the world of art and the genius of one of its teachers.

Sadly, the son of one of the families in our parish gave up his life on the mountain. He had driven there the day before the eruption planning to photograph some of her restless smoke plumes. Some of Helen's prior belches had also been quite impressive and freelance photo pickings were good. Parked directly in front of the eruption his chances for survival were nil. A few visitors on the mountain did effect miraculous escapes; regrettably, that fine young man was not one of them.

Local television clearly showed the enormity of the devastation and how great the good fortune that had been ours. There is nothing like watching one of nature's grand old dames parting with her dinner to make one realize, be it ever so humbling, how tenuous are the footsteps of man on terrain in her neighborhood.

Mount St. Helens is now a national volcanic monument. Plant and wildlife have once again established habitats. Roads are good.

New museums, superb. Tourists may now drive within hiking distance of the crater, where new facilities have been constructed at the jumping-off point. Imagine, in our lifetime and available for viewing in the visitor centers, video has captured one of Ma Nature's noble old ladies rearranging the land upon which we walk. Guests may view her handiwork on most days of the week (check with the Park Service); If desired, tourists may later visit those actual changes, close up and personal.

Thanks to Mount St. Helens' design, and the hard work of the Park Service, we have another national monument to be proud of; I think that's splendid. Further, although I am not a staunch advocate of television, too much mindless violence, in this case they truly deserve our applause.

A note of caution to visitors, seismologists have predicted that the old girl will undoubtedly grow careless and, once again, suffer through indigestion. You know what that portends!

→»   «←

Summer blew in warm and stayed long, trying to make up for winter's meanness. Our vegetable garden outdid itself, producing an abundance of sweet corn, broccoli, carrots, peas, beans, potatoes, zucchini squash, lettuce, radishes and onions — not so the tomatoes. Days were warm, but at eighteen hundred feet, nights cooled and Mojac couldn't induce the tomatoes to come to fruition. I am a tomato freak. Fix them any old way, I'll eat them and run back for more, thus those tiny green runts vexed me. One day, my Indian friend stopped by to drop off a box of his luscious looking beauties. As he lived at an even higher elevation on the Hill, I asked him how he did it? Herewith, his learned answer:

"Gather some old inner tubes and fill them with water. Stack them over the young plants, letting the bottom one rest on the ground. The sun's heat warms the water in the tubes. Each night, slip black plastic garbage bags over staked plants, be sure to also cover the warm tubes so that heat is retained. Tomatoes remain cozy and soon ripen their little selves to perfection. Note of caution. Remove bags from plants early, ere the heat of day fries them before their time."

I volunteered Mollie-O for that easy job!

That summer, while a real boon, also turned a tad brutish and she waxed too flaming hot! Standing like a forlorn derelict in a dried out waterhole, our poor waterwheel suffered. Her wood dried, cracked and split. The sheep, too lazy to use their walkover bridge, strolled the creekbed. Scratching pesky itches on the wheel's paddles, they rudely shoved, pushed, and knocked her out of joint. In despair, she finally collapsed and died. Mojac had been too busy to attend to her and arrived too late to help. Sadly, reverently, I gathered her remains and carried them over to place upon our trailer, Cuthbert. Alfred, it seemed in homage, on the way to the burn pile rolled slowly as though he were counting cadence. Upon arrival, I carefully arranged her bones on the pyre and stood for a moment of silence. In truth, I really wanted to give her a Viking's funeral, but Megan was the only dog handy and when she spied the look in my eye — she split. Is it not strange how, once they are lost, one can grieve over simple, artistically arranged, pieces of wood?

⇒≫ ≪⇐

Autumn posed prettily that year, delighting the eye. On the front lines at school, I was trying hard to invest the heads of my classroom's little poppets into fractions. Deep we were, humming, studying and learning. At least I hummed, the kids didn't like the music. Not even when I used one of my favorite examples: Your little brother took the keys to Dad's car. (They all had little brothers or sisters and considered them retarded.) Junior cannot drive (smiles all around), but the young squirt accidentally starts Pop's pride and joy. Reverse engaged, the car zooms backward out of the garage and down the driveway; enjoying the trip, it parts with a rear fender on the neighbor's fence before kissing a telephone pole! (Big chuckles here.) While in the garage the car was all in one piece, hence it was a whole object. Dad's putt-putt is now missing a fender. That fender was once part of the whole car, therefore — being one part of the whole object — it is a fraction. The denominator, a number under the fraction bar, denotes number of parts needed to form a whole object. (Blank looks.) The numerator, a number over the fraction bar, denotes number of parts of the whole object you actually have. Example: The car's parts total 50 (hypo-thetical). The back fender is one of the fifty parts — a fraction of the whole object. The fraction reads 1/50 (gentle snores.) The fender is 1/50 of the flaming car! It had been that kind of day.

Attempting to restore that fraction of my bod that had been whole, my nerves, by indulging in a small libation before dinner, Mollie-O, Megan and I were suddenly engulfed in World War III! Yelling, yelping, yodeling and gunfire resounded from the nearby twenty acres of pasture which, as Mojac was raising more sheep that year and needed extra grazing room, I had rented from my neighbor. Turning calmly to my lovely wife I said, "Dear me, there seems to be a ruckus out in yonder pasture where our pregnant sheep repose." Mollie-O says that's not what I remarked, but what do women know? I may have been a touch irked; it's hard to remember that far back.

I latched onto the shotgun and Meg and I beat feet to No Man's Land. Hunting is popular with Hill folk. Sure enough, when we strode within viewing distance, three young men, surrounded by their dogs, were busy blasting raccoons out of my rented trees!

Still calm, I asked what in the blue blazes they thought they were doing? Showing me a coon corpse reposing in the back of their pickup truck they politely replied, "Hunting. And this is doggone good raccoon country, isn't it?"

Remaining utterly calm, I informed the young gentlemen they were also trespassing, my ewes were in the family way, and I did not need twenty acres of aborted lambs! "Cease, desist and split," commanded I.

They turned out to be very nice young fellows and immedi-ately obliged, all the while apologizing for intruding. The year was 1980. I wonder — perhaps skeptically — would I be tendered that same respect today?

After checking on our expectant sheep, Megan and I, now able to enjoy the peace of a fall evening, lingered to admire the stars and listen to the wind soughing through the trees. Physically, for Mollie-O and me, the farm was a killer; aesthetically, a bit of heaven. Content at that moment in time, and also considering another minute libation, my friend, Megan, and I headed on home.

13

Meg and the Principal

Squirting on the principal is not a good principle!
Mojac

In the course of time Packy and Derm also became history and once more with the same results, full lockers and stuffed relatives. Everything has its price and saying good-bye to those two lovable clowns was painful. On the other hand, nothing can match flavor and texture of your own hand-raised vittles, be they fresh vegetables, fruit or meat. A farm is definitely a win-lose proposition. For more than a week, Megan shoved her nose in our faces, constantly questioning and searching for that duo of paddock plowers. Mollie-O left it up to me to deliver the sad news.

⇛ ⇚

At this point I am going to transport you back to Meg's fluff ball days. As you know, she was a collie canine genius. Perhaps you might like to hear a little about Megan's school days, not that she ever graduated. If truth be known, before fully crossing the threshold on her first day, Megan almost got kicked out. This is how it happened.

Whenever she became excited, Meg would immediately perform like Silver Creek's South Falls! (Reading on you will perhaps discover this chapter is overly concerned with waterfalls!). One early summer day, while Megan was still barely a handful, Mollie-O and I carried her to my school for a visit. Upon meeting the school principal, Megan promptly "splashed" onto his impeccably pressed slacks. Mortified hardly describes our discomfort. In my mind, where's a sponge? struggled with how to Houdini away. Most charitably the principal handled his flooding with courtly grace. Having been dampened many times, by his own children as well as students, he opined it was not that big a deal. Regrettably, although she had hoped to graduate bow-wow of the year, school took up in the fall sans, "Silver Falls" Megan.

MEGAN SPRINKLES

Mollie-O

Between us, Mollie-O and I have invested sixty years instructing children in classrooms, and I state this only to establish our bona fides. She has received numerous promotions and awards, "Teacher of the Year," having been already mentioned. I have been promoted and tapped for one or two kudos myself. At one time, we were both team leaders. From that, could one not perhaps deduce that Mollie-O and I might know a thing or two about teaching and its travails.

One of the agonies that besets teachers is the periodic resurrection of the ugly serpent called Merit Pay. This time the coiled reptile has been encouraged to slither forth from its basket by our own governor ... who should know better!

Merit pay is a bad idea. Not only is it unjust, but it undermines an already shaky morale. Remember, the public schools accept *all,* private schools *select.* Why is that fact so often overlooked by advocates of accountability?

Merit pay is usually fostered by agricultural chaps in the legislature. Of course, if their background is in livestock, the answer to a problem is simple, just cull 'em. With respect to the herd, once the runt, mentally deficient and the halt are eliminated, the rancher then presses on with other business.

In the classroom, the powers that be, not to mention Mom and Dad, frown on culling. And whereas the rancher would never point the finger at himself when a calf or a lamb doesn't measure up, the teacher is always the first suspect when a child doesn't learn.

If the merit pay proponent is a row crop grower, the solution is even simpler: Uniformity. Machine planted runs are even in depth, spacing and alignment. Sprinkle with water and fertilizer, add a little sun and presto, every row, every stalk, the same. The crop is uniform, each cob alike, indistinguishable one from the other. Truly there is merit in that.

But when one sprinkles fertilizer on the waiting seeds in the classroom, the program rapidly becomes a bummer. Some of the seeds like the manure. Their budding minds sway back and forth begging for seconds. Then there are those recipients, lacking gratitude, who roll the fertilizer up in a ball and throw it back! Still others, the shy, the unsure, the confused, duck behind a weed and the sprinkles never touch them.

Come harvest time, cob size and kernel growth differ from stalk to stalk. The crop is neither uniform nor identical. Considering the difficulties experienced by this grower — as punishment — should one then plant the planter?

Teachers work with *intangibles,* and these cannot be measured, unified or catalogued. Seems like folks who are chock-a-block full and eager to spread Merit Fever should first consider the vagaries of the crop being produced.

Fifteen years ago, my responsibilities as an elementary classroom teacher included instructing in spelling, writing, literature, reading, grammar, arithmetic, science, health, music, physical education (including dance), poetry, sex education, art, geography, social studies and civics, including "no to drugs." Back then, in the small rural school where I taught, my students were delightfully challenging fourth and fifth graders.

In addition to the subjects I was mandated to teach, I was an accountant, arbitrator, records keeper, lawyer, doctor, nurse, custodian and father figure. (Occasionally I was also called mother, followed by an embarrassed giggle. Not to worry, I considered that a generous compliment.) Further, I performed as psychologist, counselor, audio-visual boffin, tester, possessor of unlimited patience and an expert in child growth and development. Last but not least, I was a public relations whiz! Ever try finding a tactful way to advise Mum to trade junior in on a new model?

The requirements for my profession included the stamina of Superman together with the wisdom of Solomon. Readers, it has to be apparent that, with the exception of the greatest carpenter who ever lived, no human is an expert in all the above areas, nor can they ever hope to be. Nevertheless, society demands these qualifications in its classroom teachers. It ill behooves me to state what that same society is willing to pay for all this required expertise.

If you'll bear with me a little longer, I promise to fall off my soapbox (as I've been ordered to do by a certain pushy female party) and get back to relating about my Megan. It's just that I would really like you to hear a smattering about some of my former students.

On one particular, unforgettable day, I had a hummer of a lesson building. All thirty-two mothers' darlings were rapt, right there in the palm of my hand. I had laid the foundation, erected the walls, installed the rafters and was halfway done with the roof. This lesson was building into one of the few perfect ones in a teacher's lifetime. I soared with Socrates, free of the earth, high among approving, cottony clouds. None of my normally wriggling cherubs had made a move for the lavatory pass. Heaven was like this, I just knew it. Oh, please, let it continue.

Suddenly, a girl in the front row burst into tears! Dear Lord, what had I said? Desperately my mind began restructuring the last few sentences, seeking the cause of my little doll's outburst. I found no cause for tears.

Inwardly eyeing my masterpiece lesson, now collapsed in ruins on the classroom floor, bitterly berating my useless self, I quit blathering and quietly asked the wailing one for the source of her trouble. Damn and double damn! She related that her dog had been car-thumped that morning just prior to school bus arrival. Not knowing the current status of Bowser's health, had finally and terribly boiled over in her mind. Children are often quite cruel, they can also be most compassionate and caring. One lesson in collapse gave way to one with a desperate need. The rest of the class period was spent helping our hurting one deal with her misery.

I mention this incident because disruptions were not a rare occurrence. In some form, they happened daily. A mother or father was ill — or a brother, sister, aunt, uncle, grandmother, or grandfather. How about a sick bird, cat, goldfish or gerbil? Sometimes Mother and Dad were fighting and "Divorce!" was shouted across the dining table. Guilt and undeserved shame were by-products that showed up in my classroom. Why? The children blamed themselves. They loved them both. What to do? With a back-bowing load like that, who is concentrating on schoolwork?

So called educational experts, making their judgments from afar, and demanding educator accountability, continually overlook that already stated fact, teachers work with *intangibles!*

To equate the education of a child with the assembly of an automobile, where each part is fitted in place and in sequence, is asinine. Valid and pertinent information is presented by the instructor to the class over many days and in many ways. Name the teacher who can personally verify the knowledge now already residing in their students' heads. Sure, methods have been devised for testing, but, sadly, they are far from perfect. On any given test, the return on investment from some may be as low as ten to twenty percent.

One example: A student sleeps with his brother, who repeatedly wets the bed. The afflicted one enters school damp, aromatic and upset. Time plus schedules wait for no one. The teacher must administer those mandated exams. Count the pupil's body present, but his mind stayed home, still contending with a smelly bed! What will you bet the lad flunks the day's tests?

"Simplistic twaddle," they say. "Rare, isolated cases," cry those who have not nor ever will spend five minutes in front of a class of students, most of whom want to learn. Simplistic, rare, isolated? Baloney! Those cases — those deadly unanticipated invaders — strike the classroom week after week, month after month, all across the nation.

Part of the solution is to raise the bar for principals and other administrators. Establish a mandate that every school superintendent or principal must have a minimum of ten years actual experience — not counting student teaching — instructing in front of a class. In addition, require principals to spend two months of every year teaching in their school's classrooms and have the superintendent visit every classroom in their district at least twice a year! Those suggestions, dear reader, are not going to make me popular! Nonetheless, my reasoning is valid. Most administrators gravitate toward the money and the power — and they can't wait to get out of the classroom! A recent article in the newspaper, written by a teacher, said, "Walk a day in a teacher's shoes before you judge." In my opinion, those administrators who want to sit in judgment of a teacher's classroom performance had better have had their own lengthy teaching experience.

You are absolutely correct, what I advocate barely blows the dust off the mantel. Still, when all concerned parties are fully cognizant of classroom perils, teaching could truly become a walk of young minds through welcoming woods, sans the danger of snipers — lurking in the bushes.

Whooo-eee, this old horse has the bit in his teeth. Time to reign up. We're talking sheep and a useless dog here. Tell you what, if you'll allow me to slip in one last school anecdote, having to do with the greatest compliment I ever received during those mostly happy teaching years, I'll take you to the barn with me and let you help load the spreader with phewey-phewey.

Even at the fourth and fifth grade levels, students occasionally experience bladder problems. Each sex approaches the problem's solution differently. Boys, generally edge their chairs away from the offender, snicker, hold their noses and wait for teacher (interim Mom or Pop) to administer repairs. The teacher will usually escort the sufferer to the restroom, employ wringing-out procedures and administer needed TLC. Meanwhile, the classroom is most likely undergoing dismantling during the teacher's absence.

When the poor soul is female, the girls handle the problem quite the reverse. Once an accident occurs, one of my Thumbelinas will immediately raise her hand and say.

"Teacher, Juneth wet her panths."

I do not even blink before the maternal instinct rears her considerate head. Clucking like banty hens, three of my little mothers escort the chagrined one out the classroom door to the loo. Others grab paper towels and sop. A room mop appears, soaks up more evidence and disappears back into the closet, hopefully after rinsing! As the repair crew return to class, one of my charmers tiptoes quietly over to my desk and ever so softly, whispers,

"We washed and rinsethed her panths out and hung them up to dry. She feelths much better now."

To this day I bless their full giving hearts. Just one snort from a boy receives:

"Billy, you do that again, and Mother won't recognize you with a fat lip!"

Soft, kind, persuasive reasoning works every time with children who have a desire to live a tad bit longer.

One year, I had an eager-eyed young lady in my classroom who was frequently beset with incontinence. We all tried to cope, but her repeated floodings wore on everyone's frazzled nerves. In desperation, I requested a conference with her mother. Putting our heads together, we decided that Betsy should forget about permission or interrupting my lesson and proceed posthaste to the ladies' room whenever Niagara Falls verged on flowing in the classroom.

Happy days! The program worked a treat, until one unexpectedly damp day.

"Teacher, Betsyth's wet her panths again!"

She had been doing so well, I was disappointed and mystified by her sudden relapse. I remained totally stumped until her mother and I again conferred. Laughing, she informed me that upon taxing her daughter to explain, my delightful one had replied (I hope you're primed and ready for this!),

"I didn't forget. I knew I should have left for the bathroom, but the lesson was so interesting and different, I didn't want to leave the room for just a few more minutes." Now that is what I call MERIT PAY!

Unless we wish to imperil riches held dear never forget to whom the future belongs. Give the kids a break. Society's in a flaming sweat for them to grow up, and equally determined on sliding them all into a mailbox sporting a one-size-slot. Why? Is it unthinkable for children to laze away a warm friendly day gazing up at soft clouds created for dreaming? I wish I understood why it's imperative to rob them of childhood. The danger's in forgetting that children feel. Robots are tin machines performing tasks without feeling. I detest any like them.

Aside from marriage, my greatest happiness in life has been teaching, working with, and enjoying our bright, engaging, glorious young. And of course, Megan, who hopes your chosen vocation will likewise be a posy of four-leaf clovers, and equally as rewarding.

-≫   ≪-

We lost Megan once again when she was not quite a year old. Our friend got an education in the perils of foot loose wandering that time, although we never did find out for certain who did the teaching. She answered to Meg the Roamer then, as she liked to visit the neighbors. Farm fencing presented no obstacle to Megan, she could eel through or climb over anything standing between her and freedom. Peppy was a stay-at-home dog, primarily because he never could figure out a way to scarper. Neither dog was kept penned when Mojac was home, which allowed them plenty of opportunity for exercise and escapades.

Megan liked to be petted, hugged and fussed over, she did not like weighty nose to nose confrontations. I nosed our AWOL kid like butter on hot toast! Collaring her ruff I pulled her sniffer, body attached, to within two inches of my own. I then proceeded to seriously discuss the situation with her.

"Dear little Meg, you will not skinny through or over fences, visit neighbors, or leave these premises without permission. Is that clear?"

Megan got the message. Trouble was she paid no attention to it. As a consequence, one Saturday she turned up missing. When a search of the farm turned up no trace of her, Mollie-O cranked up the truck and left to search the byways. A fair distance down the highway lived a family with two young boys. Mollie-O stopped to inquire. Mom and Dad were absent and the youngsters denied any knowledge of Megan's whereabouts. As Mollie-O restarted the truck, one of the young lads hollered, "And why did you shoot our dog?"

Shoot their dog! As previously stated the only thing I desired shooting was the tax collector. A puzzling question indeed. Mojac had never even seen their dog.

A missing Border collie. A false accusation. A fruitless search. A growing suspicion. That Saturday became more confusing and frustrating by the flaming minute. Our voices were hoarse from calling, but no answers were forthcoming.

Returning to the farm, Mollie-O helped me tend to chores, interspersed with further calls for Megan — the one who will surely get it when and if she ever shows up! Two hours later, tail between her legs, a "forgive me" look on her face, Megan scampered onto Mojac like the prodigal who had really only been kidding about leaving the security of her loving, comforting abode.

Where had she been? A guess off the top of my phrenological head. I think the kids — as retribution for our imaginary crime — had her stashed when Mollie came inquiring. When Mom and Dad returned from shopping and found the stashee, they made the little kidnappers spring her. I do not think they had thumped on her, but she was one subdued dog. Regardless, Megan's straying days were over. From then on Meg the Roamer became Meg the Mojac Hermit. She never went anywhere without us.

The only other time she escaped confinement, she didn't wander far. During the school week, she and Peppy were penned up together. Being good pals, they were quite content to be with one another. However, Miss Megan was nothing if not adventuresome. Putt-putting into the yard one evening we found her on the front patio. Wagging her tail, while at the same time belly-crawling guiltily, she barked, "See how clever I am, I got out all by myself." While trying not to laugh, we spoke sternly to her and she added, "You guys aren't really mad, are you? I stayed right here on the front porch, by myself, all day long."

Was I ticked? Naw! I just installed a controlled movement roaming line between two widely spaced trees in their pen, allowing freedom of travel yet denying her access to the fence. Consequently, Alcatraz experienced no more break-outs. The prodigal — well and truly hoosegowed — became a permanent homebody. Peppy, no longer jealous, was happy. Cats, no longer scattered by a truant collie, peacefully drowsed the days away, and were happy. The mailman, new uniform tatter free, was happy. The oilman, free of a pesky hitch-hiker, smiled long and often. Was Megan happy? Who cares! I was happy!

⇛   ⇚

How long can happiness last? Three weeks later, heading to the barn to dole out the nightly feed, I inadvertently left open the gate to the orchard. I went via the wellhouse pasture when returning to the house, as I wanted to check the number of days service we'd had on the light bulb. As it was a balmy, rain-free evening, once the sheep had eaten, they strolled out into the paddock. Spying the open gate, and curious, the whole flock waltzed into the orchard. In addition to our fruit trees, we had also planted five rows of fir trees, which were now two to three years old. Lush new growth on the branch tips appealed to the trespassing sheep. Excuse the pun, they pigged out! Stepping up onto the front porch preparatory to entering the house, I heard an unusual noise emanating from the orchard. I hastened to check and when I spotted the intruders, I hollered for Meg. Together, we proceeded to run them out and back to the barn. Till then, even though barricades had been erected around pasture trees, I'd no idea sheep would eat evergreen needles. After securing the orchard gate and taking a last look around the farm, I stopped off once more to check the flock.

Lord God above! They were all groaning and literally foaming at the mouth. I just knew they'd poisoned themselves on those trees and were well on the way to dying. Mollie-O called the vet. I wrung my hands and watched the sheep. The groaning and foaming increased. Frantic, I tried to think of something to try which would relieve their misery. What was the antidote for fir tree poison?

After an eternity (trust me!) the vet showed up and took a gander at Mojac's groaning woollies.

"What I think we have here is a gigantic case of sheepish bellyache," he said, "like a bunch of little kids who've been eating green apples. It's the resin in the fir needles causing the problem and I don't have anything that will help. If you folks are living right, in a mite more time, they should snap out of it themselves. We'll just stand here and watch awhile."

An agonizing twenty minutes later, a few quit foaming and then, groaning. A half-hour more and they all began to look bright-eyed once again. Soon, they all headed for the water tub, drank deep and long, returned to their straw beds, settled down, and chewed their cud. Oh, yeah, raising sheep was a laugh a minute, like discovering, on your first jump, the parachute is on backwards!

14

Meg and the Attack Cats

Caterwaul, spit, scratch; Megan has met her match!
Mojac

Megan elevated belly-crawling to an art form, displaying it always at inopportune moments. To her list of nicknames, I added the moniker Psycho Dog — not because she was crazy, she simply drove everyone else nuts! Invariably, Meg would perform her WBC (woebegone belly-crawl) routine when visitors were present. Mollie-O and I never laid a hand on her, but her little act used to fire up my Irish. Oh sure, once in a great while I might raise my voice, but it was more like a dulcet yodel — "Meg-o-o-o-o-o" — never a full-blown roar! Nevertheless, check out her immediate WBC. Potential customers would stiffen, accuse me with their eyes of being a canine-beating bully, and vacate the premises. This did not help our much needed Mojac lamb or sheep sales.

Visitors gone, solitude reigning once more, Miss Megan would look up at me with those gorgeous brown eyes — laugh — and trot off to bug the cats.

Ready, in her customary spot in the back of the Buick, Megan awaits Mojac's regular Sunday excursion to church. After the service, myself having vowed to sin no more, I would always free Meg for a quick run. After she had attended to the necessaries, I'd call most softly, "Meg-o-o-o-o-o."

Showtime!

In plain view of the entire congregation, she'd bring her WBC to the fore. Frowning worshippers would stare, nudge a neighbor and whisper, "Will you look at that cruel bum! And he just attended Mass! Oh, the poor, dear, mortified little doggie!"

Satisfied, Psycho Dog would grin, jump into the rear of the wagon, and wait for the rest of the Mojac clan to quietly board and then slink guiltily out of the churchyard. One of these days, Alice, ... POW!

⇒》   《⇐

When Mojac first purchased the farm, the joint was overrun with felines. Squeaky, a sweet, friendly Persian, bossed the rest of the brethren. Rusty wore a short coat, nondescript in color. Blackie, a big cat, with some white markings, had a gentle disposition. A rat-faced sucker named You're Really Ugly made himself scarce every time we set foot in his bailiwick, which encompassed the entire fourteen and a half acres. Soon after our arrival, Rusty and You're Really Ugly split for good, which cut our mousing crew in half. Must have been something I said.

Blackie, in the way of all cats, was a roamer. I once spotted him curled up in one of the ill-fated raccoon trees, way out in our rented pasture, "Blackie!" I bellowed. "Better breeze yer buns barnward before boulders be bouncing off yer black bod! Mice are partying back home, not up that tree." Hastening to comply, he yawned, stood, turned three times and lay back down on a softer branch.

Some four years into our stint at Mojac Farm, on one blissful catnip-odor day, Blackie, ignoring Squeaky's sage advice, pawed jauntily off to check out the kitty cat action across the highway. Unfortunately, a strawberry laden truck interfered with his stroll and he never completed that trip.

With Rusty, and You're Really Ugly, hoboing the Hills, and Blackie plucking strings with the angels, our barn patrol was now reduced to a single feline, Squeaky. One day during our summer layoff, he also disappeared.

We searched for him for over a week. Megan frantically nosed all his favorite haunts, nary sign, nary meow. His milk dish remained untouched until Peppy lazered an eye on it, whereupon the contents suddenly vanished, as slick as a wallet picked from a pocket at a county fair.

Glorious workday after glorious workday rushed by until, entering the barn to feed the stock eight days later, who should Meg and I spy but the immortal Squeaky sitting in a patch of sunshine washing his face!

I was so flaming glad to see the old boy that I picked him up, ran to the house, opened the front door and hollered, "Mollie-O, here's a surprise for you!" Unintentionally then, I came down with a case of the bozo stupids and I tossed him — gently mind you — onto the floor of the hallway. He landed on his left foreleg and his nose and let out a louder than usual Squeaky squall. Thinking nothing of it, Megan and I headed back to continue enjoying chores.

The sweet old guy had been washing a hurt paw, not his face! Mollie-O told me later his right foreleg was badly injured; apparently he had been holed up in the barn loft in and back of the hay bales nursing that hurt for eight days. We have no idea what he ate or drank all that time, but he sure made a quart of milk disappear — toot swallow!

Trying to deduce, I figured Squeaky had been rafter hopping after scooting mice, lost his balance, jumped for a support beam, jammed his paw in the join, twisted in midair and — finally wrenching free — had fallen to the loft floor, whereupon he crawled into the hay, hoping to die. That's only a guess, I couldn't get a word out of him.

Our Vet diagnosed damaged muscles, severely torn tendons and ligaments, but no broken bones. Unfortunately, the damage was irreparable. Squeaky became a tri-legged (carry one and work three) cat. I dubbed him The Gimp.

Figuring he'd paid his dues, Squeaky surrendered the barn to the bleeding mice and opted for well earned retirement. Except for an occasional left hook to a couple of canine noses, he was content to laze around on Mojac Social Security. Hallelujahs from Rodentville. Purrs from The Gimp. Our need for feline reinforcements was obvious, a songster well versed in Faustian librettos. Sort of a tuck-me-in and nighty-night crooner to those celebrating mice! Accordingly, the necessity to visit yon cattery became immediate.

Parents of one of my little squashes housed a surplus of kittens, I was told they were weaned and ready to enjoy farm life. Gassing the Buick, Mojac headed to town for a look-see.

Superdog was ninety-nine percent mistake proof. Hosanna hammer that bell though, when she did err it was bound to be a door knocker heard all over the valley! That eventful day burned summer warm, so, entering el gato's owners' driveway, our wagon's windows were open. Bad news! Kittens' momma was a tough old broad. Check that, she was a grimalkin killing machine; purringly happy only when offing dogs — any size! While I inspected our possible new calico contralto, answering to Bandit, Momma Cat planted her paws on the wagon's side door and called Meg a dirty name. Megan responded in kind. Whereupon, amenities then suspended, real insults were exchanged resulting in Herself being invited outside to a put up or shut up party! A certain Border — lacking the brains God gave a duck — floated groundward through the open window thinking to browbeat mother with mouth and muscle.

Lordy, lordy, 'twas a mistake. Such a big mistake! That feral, feline assassin proceeded to take Meg apart! A sublime day for that cat was a stack of canine bodies for the kittens to play with. Snarling, squalling, hissing and growling, drowned out the singing of birds, the hum of insects, the gentle soughing of a summer breeze through the trees. Peace no longer lived here.

Well, of course, while I galloped all over the flaming yard chasing the hunted and the hunter, in an effort to effect separation and rescue, the kitten occupied herself by shredding my arm. I feared to drop her, deeming it prudent to not raise the ire of Momma Cat any higher. Finally — on my third circuit of the yard — I stuffed the tiny beast into her owner's arms, quickly checked for a spurting artery and then, once again, took off after Stand and Fight, and Bail

Me Outa Here. At last, stretching my remaining arm three inches longer than it actually was, I collared Meg, threw her into the back of the wagon and cranked up the windows. So what if she did suffocate! Meanwhile, Murder Inc. placed her front paws high up on the side door and hurled threats as fast as she could invent them. Megan turned her back on the old crone, lay down and sulked.

Mine hostess, after she quit laughing, penned Megan's nemesis and then pinned my arm back together. Mojac bid a fond farewell to "Momma" and enfolding Bandit (in future, Bandita), cozy-like in a towel, cranked up the Buick and highwayed away to our peaceful farm. The vanquished kept her back to us, uttered not one bark, and pouted all the way home.

I calculated that Bandita, being related to that feline fee-fa-fum, was a cinch to grab on to Carmen's best arias and tidbit herself royally on Mojac's mice choir. In reality, she became monarch of the whole spread, held friendly relations with Miss Megan, and turned out to be another farm sweetheart. Ten years later we are still providing room and board to one of her offspring, Muffy by name. Grandmother (killer cat) would really hate it — but he's a dedicated pacifist.

Strangely, a month later, with his funny little — hinge needs oil — mew, his old bones no longer capable of mice snagging jumps, our beloved Squeaky yowled, staggered and lurched over to his Mollie-O. He died in her arms the victim of a fatal heart attack.

Oregon's motto: "alis volat propriis" aptly memorializes Mojac's knight of the realm, Sir Squeaky. We miss him.

⇒⟫   ⟪⇐

Megan suffered another attack cat experience seven years later. After a visit to Los Angeles (including Disneyland — laugh if you will), we swung south to San Diego and talked Davey into coming back with us for another Oregon visit. Mature beavers, alias ex sheep farmers, tire sooner than younger ones so we elected to overnight in Paso Robles.

Stretching our legs after dinner, we three and Meg strolled by a furniture store supporting a massive picture window. Megan, admiring the display along with us, bumped her nose on the glass.

LEMME
OUTA
HERE!

OPEN M. — S.
9 A.M. — 6 P.M.

Mellie-O

In the blink of an eye, like a super-charged bolt of lightning, a huge tailless attack cat, snarling and spitting, slammed into and bounced off the glass on the room side of the window. Unfazed and intent on Meg, this deadly serious dynamo, belted the glass again.

The three of us were startled into involuntary backward leaps into the middle of the road. Although the glass appeared to be quite strong, Megan, before the next attack, visualizing another Border collie annihilation, was down the street, into the motel and under the bed before our three pairs of petrified feet had carefully tip-toed past the building's end, free of the killer's sight. As I relate this brief but traumatic tale, I state, unequivocally, Attila was even meaner than Bandita's momma! Fear not, as we trekked on the next day, except for a perpetual shiver every time she saw a cat, Megan prettied along, her old bouncy — bug 'em all — self.

⇒》 《⇐

It was the onset of Summer Layoff and for a change, some time was available to Mojac for the unusuals. One day, while grinding leftover winter alfalfa for evening feed, Molly called me up from the barn to take a decidedly different phone call. The caller was interested in purchasing one of our ram lambs for her eleven-year-old nephew, residing in Arizona. The boy was involved in 4H and desired a young ram to train and show at the state fair in Phoenix. Would we be willing to ship one of our little guys south and a mite east via air freight?

Full of doubt, I tried to explain that the boy could buy a ram cheaper, and perhaps as good (which I didn't believe for one flaming minute!), right there in Arizona. Price of a Mojac lamb, plus crating, handling, vet fees and shipping would be costly. Having never transported sheep by air before, I could not guarantee live delivery. We were proud of our sheep, and I didn't want to put one of the young rams at risk. Despite all my arguments to the contrary, I ran into firm resolve, the caller insisted that she still wanted one of our rams.

No farmer likes to turn down a sale. The line of buyers clamoring at the gate is not exactly long. Yet, send a lamb to — Arizona? Finally I decided, why not? Is not the quality of our flock, high? Do not airplanes fly (most of the time)? One Mojac lamb she wanted, one Mojac lamb she would flaming well have!

Reminiscent of the year when E. Flynn first distinguished himself, we just happened to have a couple of gosh-awful, good-lookin', purebred ram lambs we had had the smarts to hang onto. The two had shown promise at birth, and both were in a race for first place in Mojac's — Handsome and Then Some — gallery.

Megan cut them out of the flock of wethers we were fattening and walked the two darlin's into the barn. After penning them, examining and taking measurements, I chose one, ribboned him, and then Megan carefully returned both to pasture.

Next, I trucked on down to the lumberyard and explained what would be needed and why. Too many har-har-hars from salesman accompanied my order. Wiseguy! Wheeze back up the hill to You're Out of Your Mind Acres, and begin assembly of the ram flight pen by promptly belting thumb with hammer! Women, by nature, are nosy, so of course Mollie-O wanted to know why all the pirouetting, she darn well knows I can't dance. After a lengthy glare, Megan and I suggested, as we builders were busy and had no time for chit-chat, that she go and weed the skunk cabbage! Why is it that slams on one's appendages with metal objects hurt so blamed much and last so blamed long?

Construction proceeded without further crippling clouts, and by the next day, swank, first class, ram lamb digs were complete.

Next, schedule appointment with vet for traveler's exam and preflight shots, then book ram's flight on airline and cable recipient of impending lamb arrival.

Flight day dawned sunny and warm. Handsome Lad trod docilely into his first class accommodation — and promptly stuck his head through the slats! We were due at the vet's in twenty minutes. Desperately, I grabbed my favorite maiming tool and some nails. I measured, cut more slats and then set to, while constantly reassuring the crate's puzzled occupant, "Mind moving your head back, Li'l Bopeep? I'm not terribly skilled with this dome-denter. OOPS — I am truly sorry, was that an ear?" An anxious look at my watch. Bang. One more bar nailed. Whack. On goes the next one. Another swing ... , "Ah, gee, your poor foot must be really smarting, never mind, a dab of liniment and you'll be as good as new."

Precious minutes later our ram was so well barred he couldn't poke an eyelash through to freedom. At last, only ten minutes late for our appointment with the vet, Mojac motored down the highway.

During the Doc's examination, our ram fledgling flyer, quite nervous by now, proceeded to decorate him; considering what the vet was charging for the shot, I figured that a fair exchange. Clutching lamb's health certificate, one eye on my watch, the other on the road, I gunned the Dodge onto the freeway. Portland Airport, look out — Mojac Farm is going to make your day!

With fifteen precious minutes to spare before takeoff, I backed the pickup up to the air cargo dock. An official type, duded up in arrogance and citing chapter and verse, informed me that freight, alive or dead, had to be processed at the veddy least, one hour before takeoff. Already leaning toward Mount Hectic, considering what we had already been through to get to the airport at all, does Mojac need this? I glared what I thought of his flaming pedigree at him. Condescendingly, he decided to accept Mojac's sheep shipee.

The final paperwork completed, Mollie-O, Meg and I bade farewell and happy trails to Handsome Lad and tootled off for a nerve-calming libation (ice cream for the pooch). A leisurely two hours later, back at Mojac, we to and froed nervously on the patio swing awaiting the confirmation of arrival telephone call from the Phoenix Airport. Well, I will tap both feet and do a heel and toe, our ram landed smack on the nose and — a-okay.

By and by, autumn colored in and a newspaper clipping arrived in the mail. At the Arizona State Fair, in Phoenix, the youngster had won first place for novice showmanship and Handsome Lad had won the blue ribbon for yearling ram! Hey, what can I say, what else could he do, after all, his poppa was E.Flynn, and you also know what he could do!

CHAMPIONS
ALL

15

Meg and Frisbee

A whiz by the ear, could a frisbee be here?

Mojac

When faithful Peppy laid claim to eight years, a black cloud descended on Mojac Farm. Flying over field and farm one day, Peppy suddenly skidded on his fanny into a fence. Large dogs are susceptible to bone problems; dear old Peppy had pranged himself due to that old bugaboo, major hip displacement. He stood up, a puzzled look on his face, as if saying to the sheep, "Which of you bleeding blatters tripped me?" The vet prescribed rubdowns and muscle relaxants. Slow, careful walks, a special diet, and extra TLC became the order of the day. Nothing worked. Peppy — our gentle giant — grew steadily, debilitatingly worse.

Teaching consumed our days now, necessitating the penning of both dogs while we were away. The classroom demanded long hours and we never arrived home early. Even though he was free to roam within the confines of their enclosure, if Peppy were to collapse and then be unable to rise, he would suffer terribly for lack of water until our return. Megan could be of no help to her beloved friend. Inevitably, deplorably — we had to put him down.

Another spate of pain for Mojac. Every death on the farm hurt, but the loss of Peppy truly devastated. Megan was inconsolable. Her lifelong best friend had gone and she could not understand why. Her expressive brown eyes radiated grief. When Mollie-O and I provided company, she coped; but the long, lonely days by herself were pure torment.

When we arrived home at night, Megan, happy to see us, seldom whined, cried or barked. Instead, she would spring straight off the ground, all four feet at once, her version of a canine jack-in-the-box. The height of those leaps, and subsequent shortage of oxygen, would have caused my nose to bleed. Released from confinement, she would imitate a whirling dervish, in headlong pursuit of her tail. Straightening, she would race away like a lifer at long last granted parole. Sadly, and having no recourse, next morning she'd once again been incarcerated behind bars.

What does a bored and pining Border collie do when she is alone? They don't get mad, they get even. Megan put her mind to work, then busier than a wrecking crew knocking a landmark down, proceeded to dismantle the garage wall which served as one side of her pen! Returned home, after a long wearing day with my little sneezers, I found long strips of siding strewn all over the pen's floor, and a smile on Meg's face, which upon interpreting, read, "Poke that up your nose — buddy! Care to leave me on my lonesome again?"

Forced to either remove doggie's teeth in order to retain a standing garage, or find a quick solution, I wracked my brain, snuck into Mollie-O's purse, stole her allowance, shopped at the lumber yard, cried over the prices and finally, metal sided the pen's wooden wall. Try that on the old molars, Meg me dear!

⇒≫   ≪⇐

I am a night person. One who delights in the enchanting pageantry of the setting sun. Present me a roaring fire, where shadows play on the wall, and I'll spend hours in front of it. You know I'm not a morning person. I have no interest whatsoever in propping my eyelids open with toothpicks simply to watch the sun struggling to rise; to this day my body hasn't forgiven me for submitting it to such cruel and unusual punishment, just for the silly purpose of photographing dawn breaking over Monument Valley — although I did capture some prize worthy shots.

When I stagger out of bed in the morning, noon, or whenever, I'm in dire need of a hot cup of coffee, while I consider the merits (if any) of continuing to live.

Megan wasn't perfect! She had absolutely no compassion for those who would sleep late. I'll prove my point. Other than her woebegone belly crawl which has already been illustrated, her most irritating habit answered to the aggravating title of, ACNOABA (A cold nose on a bare arm)!

As punctual as winter flooding, Megan, desiring my attention, would pad silently into the kitchen, and always from the blind side, reach out and repeatedly butt my arm with her blunt, icicle nose. In my semi-comatose morning condition, this greeting was comparable to being nudged by a frozen prune left to thaw on a refrigerator shelf overnight. If you've never experienced a hot coffee shower or seen Folger's dripping from the ceiling, then you've never had breakfast with Megan. I much prefer my coffee quietly steaming inside the cup.

Long sleeve shirt weather brought some relief from Megan's cold nose greeting, but her "notice me" good morning jolt, still sent a shot of Mollie-O's tasty lava java straight up my nose. On the plus side, my sinuses remained quiescent.

For sixteen years, Megan thoroughly enjoyed her nudgy little ritual — and drove me to distraction. How come I kept going to Dumb School? Why couldn't a cagey school teacher outsmart a dog? After all, I out-conned the kids in my classroom all the time, right? Try to ignore the pitiful sight of a grown man in tears and believe me when I say, "I tried."

It became a daily game with the mangy cur. If I switched and drank southpaw, she would butt me from the left. When I allowed my coffee to table-sit, trying to wait her out, she withdrew her frigid schnoz and watched my rejuvenator grow cold. Aroma, heat and taste had to be approximately three inches from desperately reaching lips — before glacier-nose would strike again. You suggest, "Why not try strong chamomile?" No good. Hot tea raining from the ceiling, tea bag up my nose. "Iced tea?" What a great idea, except there for some reason, she left me alone. I hate iced tea!

Consolation had I but one. Every time she zapped me, my first impulse was to grab hold of her Adam's apple and squeeze out a pint of cider. I never did, man of peace that I am, but oh how I reveled in that fantasy.

⇒⟫ ⟪⇐

Whenever dabs of time became available to steal, Megan and I would hunt up a comfortable spot to fanny-park and watch the goings-on around the farm. Stump sitting, as long as we kept still, Meg and I could then enjoy eyeing animal behavior. I'm convinced our Mojac frogs bordered on brilliant!

I remember one droughty year in particular when many Hill streams and even ponds dried up. The farm's lesser springs had ceased to flow, however, our swimming hole still retained an ample supply of water. A short hop from Meg's pond there lay a small wading hollow. Mojac's amphibious croakers happily congregated around it for the social hour. During a further study period, Megan and I observed that the damp of Happy Hour Hollow now blew dust, and our frogs seemed somewhat perturbed. The parching weather continued. A few days later, again contented observers, Megan and I were astonished to discover that the dried out froggy's hot tub was once more awash and brimful of water.

Most curious," warbled I, "Mayhap a spring hast sprung." I beg to report, negative on a liberated spring, and the next day the pool blew powder again. By now, Mojac cast imploring eyes skyward looking for some hope of precipitation (can you beat it, begging for rain in Oregon!).

A full week of dry hollow/wet hollow passed before, on another dry day, Megan solved the mystery. Nobbling me with her nose she pointed out a long line of frogs hopping from her grand pond toward their happy hour gathering hole. Twenty-two rather chubby amphibians then lined up straight in one row, and all spitting at the same time — flooded the hollow like a cloudburst topping a rain barrel! Now tell me they aren't brilliant.

Whoops! I think I hear Mollie-O's dulcet voice calling us to lunch. Think she'll believe what we've just seen, Meg?

FROG HOLLOW

Chewing on all that dust carried Megan and me back a few years to when Mojac rented the extra pasture. The need for water there was a problem, too. Meg's pond lay within our fences and since that field needed a rejuvenating rest, the leased twenty acres lacked a source of water. Fortunately, I could always call upon Chesley! He was a huge, old, boiler tank attached to the frame of a trailer mounted on truck tires which, slow leakers, were always in need of pumping up. His frame narrowed and joined at the front whereupon resided another hitch, which just happened to fit the ball on Alfred. Separated by acetylene torch, half an old water heater formed the water trough; it had been securely welded in front of Chesley's tank and onto his frame. A faucet had been welded into a drilled hole in the lower center of the boiler above the trough and slowly dripped water.

When Alfred towed Chesley's water filled tank to the rented acres, Megan kept our inquisitive sheep away from all opened gates. Alfred and I chugged on by, up a hill and into a grove of sheltering oak trees, where I unhitched, leveled and braced Chesley and his precious cargo. Tank secured, I'd open the faucet, fill the trough, adjust tap for a slow drip, and then holler to Megan to let the sheep come and drink.

For some reason on those sojourns, I always felt like a Basque shepherd. I fancied myself Gilbert Roland, complete with serape, tam, six-gun and his faithful dog, Megan, bravely guarding the flock against sheep rustlers and other thieves. I would camp among my charges and cook beans for my dinner. That idea always brought me out of my reverie, I detest beans! Quickly back in the land of reality, Megan and I would urge the woollies to enjoy the water and some pleasant grazing. Then we would head for home and let Mollie-O cook supper. Seemed fair!

⇒≫   ≪⇐

Two years after the arrival of our six calves, Mojac ended up perched on the horns of a dilemma. One Horn Willy and his five buddies had grazed Crazy Acres into a state of sparseness. Ours was a small spread and six steers could and did decimate pasture in a cud chewing hurry.

Making matters worse, they left behind prodigious, preponderating pats of processed patooie. The day I received a requisition from the sheep for stilts, something purely had to give.

Like so many things Mojac did to excess, we fell into cattle raising unaware of costs, complexities and labor. As a result of the demise and distribution of Filet and Mignon, kinfolk had developed a stampeding taste for fresh, farm-raised meat. Soon, subtle suggestions from near and far — flying on the wind — fluttered through a Mojac window to whisper, "Why don't you and Mollie-O raise some more calves along with your sheep? Goodness knows, you've plenty of room. Once they stand high off the ground, we will each buy one. How's that for a good deal?"

Good deal for whom? The relatives lived in suburban bliss. What about Mojac? They bought, fed, doctored, and during winter squalls, mucked out the rapidly filling cattle barn — continuously! Inevitably, Willy and his boys grew. Mucking out, taking longer, becomes harder and mire is now up and over Megan's elbows.

Bleating (not from the sheep) telegraphed in night letter to relatives, from Mojac. "Steers grown pretty big now. Much trouble to care for. Time for adios. How soon you pony up promised bread, and also rent locker for your beef?"

Answer from loved ones: "Oh, we couldn't possibly use a whole steer! No, no, no. But we do desire a hindquarter. Steaks, roasts, ribs and stew meat will do nicely, forget the hamburger. Surely you can quite easily arrange that!"

Soft reply cabled to untrustworthy members of flaming family: "I've got blisters on me palms, a bow to me back, not one foot of ground where I can safely place me sliding feet, and all you want is the choicest of the meat?"

At the break of day, an irked Mojac called a cattle buyer, and at a loss, sold five large dogies — to go. We kept One Horn Willy. Why not? Once, I'd been ever so close to becoming permanently attached to him.

One more telegram to kinfolk: "In future, please feel free to patronize your local Defrost and Watch it Curl market and avail yourselves of the opportunity to purchase their meat!"

Moral of steer pat story: Next time a cousin hollers, "Where's the beef?" Upside his head with your hoof!

⇒⇒ ⇐⇐

Mojac had now been sheep farming for over seven years and a major problem had to be faced, a decision made. With all the experience we had gained shoveling manure, you would've thought we'd be prepared to deal with more. Not so.

It seems some ivory-towered IRS tax technician devised a rule that a business venture has to show a profit. If, perusing the books on the venture registered as Hernia Heaven, said business venture fails to show a profit within seven years, listed enterprise shall be deemed a hobby. Hobbies, or pastimes as they are known in the trade, may not, shall not and will not deduct expenses. Not satisfied with the shirt off my back, the IRS now desires to lay claim to my one and only pair of pants.

Just once, I'd like to lock a few of those pencil-pushing pharisees in the barn, and let them hand load phewey-phewey until their eyes popped. A hobby? My stove in back! How can a bureaucrat decree that a business must show a profit? Who can predict the economy today, tomorrow, next week? Who can control drought, famine, inflation and pestilence — or predict a buyer's whim?

Where is it ordained, if the working man ever reaps an extra buck, it is the prerogative of those poly pundits to nose around in his pocket like hogs rooting for truffles? A small farm: hobbies for the rich — bad jokes for the poor.

Regardless, fair or no, having arrived at number two thousand seven hundred and fifty plus days — over seven years — the tax bell tolled for Mojac.

Our teachers' salaries couldn't support a livestock hobby. Unable to show a penny of profit, the time had come for Mojac to part with their beloved sheep.

Occasionally, luck also just might run the other way. We found a kind, loving family willing to provide a home and care for our flock. Knowing our innocents would be well treated made saying good-bye one sniff less painful.

On the appointed day, watching the truck haul our children away through the final pasture gate, we stood with our arms entwined straining for one last sight, and bawling like little kids who had just stubbed their toes on the first day of a shoeless summer. When she thought no one was looking, I caught Megan also gulping hard to hold back the big ones.

One night, a week after the silence of a no stock farm was driving me round the bend, I had a humdinger of a dream: IRS (pronounced "iris") and I were husband and wife. Naturally, being married to IRS it has been a sentence of many long years. In addition, truly living up to her name, she was the dominant partner and meanly dictated how much money I'd have to spend, and exactly how I would spend it.

One dismal day, I believe it was April 15th, after filling Chumley, the spreader, with one final load of phewey-phewey, old and worn down to a nubbin — I died! Not being totally reprehensible, I find myself standing before the Pearly Gates awaiting entrance. St. Peter, after checking my papers and finding them in order tells me I have but to spell one word and then I may enter. The word is LOVE. How tough can that be? I spell it and — bingo — I'm in. It was a slack time at the gate, all the freeway maniacs were blocked by mud slides, so I lingered awhile to chat with Peter. We nattered about wool prices, lambing and the market. Of course he was more into fish, but I've discovered people of soil and sea have no trouble gabbing about meaningful topics. He knew a great deal on the subject of lambing.

After a bit he told me of an important meeting all the older resident angels have been called to, and would I tend the gate in his absence. Nervously, I nod yes, but the request immediately reaches out and piques my nosy bones. Wasn't I in Heaven? Heaven is perfect, right? Here we have no crime, no sin, no politics. What problem could possibly call for a major gathering of the winged and saintly? I just had to ask St. Peter, why the need for a confab? Here is what he told me:

"Management, which means everybody up here, has bumped into a small dilemma that, occurring in Heaven, naturally has to do with feathers. It seems a micro chip in a traffic control box at the intersection of Neighborly Way and Brotherly Love has gone bananas. Instead of flashing red and green, the lights flash all colors of the rainbow. Stop signs, state of the art neon, no longer read, 'Thou wilt stoppeth.' All four corners, now brazen in vulgar magenta, simultaneously blink, "Goeth for it!" Ye stop boxes' micro chips reek of brimstone!"

"Naturally, we have shopping malls in Paradise, really classy, offering beluga caviar, high-tech harps, down-filled angel gowns, golden chimes and, nary a dollop of cholesterol, Big Mac's to piggest out on. All gratis. It flat boggles the angelic mind!"

"Angels don't always fly, sometimes they use handy, no smog, cloud shuttles, floating sidewalks, and even shanks' mare. Unfortunately, a former diva coming from the east along Neighborly Way, intent on grabbing the last, gigantic-size, down-gown at I. Magnin's, heeded the stop sign's new message and barreled right through the intersection. Built like a 747, she creamed a Marine named Allison, himself no lightweight, who was escorting a cute little nun across the street on Brotherly Love. She knocked him arse over teakettle. Result, both of them lost some wing feathers. No big deal. True, the mezzo can no longer fly to Milan to angelically voice support for her successor, in Carmen. Marine Allison cannot fly to his favorite island for the continuing thrill of dismantling those big guns. Still, a dab of bag balm, an ice bag and a few aspirin would have smoothed things out and put paid to the problem."

"Unfortunately, here is where the whole mess turned devilish. King Poi-Poi, happening to be in the vicinity when the diva clobbered the Marine, picked up both the crash victim's feathers, and though offered a special luau as a reward, he wouldn't give them back."

"Why ever not?" I asked.

"This is why," said Peter.

"When that famed warrior, cosmic called, crossed the frontier 'tween heaven and earth, a metal detector panicked, and two border guards wouldn't let him pass until he surrendered his headdress. Now Poi-Poi was real proud of that beany. He had wired rare, imported, whydah feathers to pikake vine, it was one of a kind. 'You speaketh for the devil in forked tongues. My bonnet is big medicine, and detector or no detector, I'll see you in hell before I'll give it up!' Holding all the aces (guess who already sported asbestos wings?), that zorilla duo didn't buy the King's threat. 'No headdress — no Heaven,' they replied, refusing his invitation to get fired up."

"No one gets too many chances at Paradise, so Poi-Poi, unloaded some nasty Kanaka cuss words, lowered his war club and surrendered his beany."

"As a result," said Simon Peter, "The king has been looking for loose feathers for a new bonnet ever since. A famous warrior is nothing without honor, dignity and headdress, but the Boss only hands out one set of wings per customer. You lose 'em, bend 'em, or dent 'em, and walking ain't crowded. Hopefully a flocking together of angels won't foul things up any worse, but we have to convince King Poi-Poi to give the feathers back. Now, will you tend the gate for me?"

"It will be my pleasure. What would you have me do?" I inquire.

"Admit prospects exactly as I've been doing, and be sure our future angels spell that sublime, all encompassing word, LOVE, ere you let them enter."

With that, Peter hopped aboard a local shuttle and aired away to the angels important, fuss and feathers meeting. Piece of cake! I can handle this little old celestial gate.

Soon, two hopeful prospects show up: Ka-boi-n-n-g! Smack in the middle of her 10,000th mortgage foreclosure, the banker's heart had tick-tocky, ding-donged a sudden and final, "buenas noches amiga." The other — a tax lawyer — had just figured out how to triple tax a widow, or widower, when the other helpmate shuffled off. Regrettably, three days of prolonged applause from his colleagues proved too much for his clock and the mainspring, performing the Zulu Stomp without a license, pranged, poked a hole in his electric plant's generator and his time ran out. Neither one had ever heard of the word love, let alone knew how to spell it. I ran them both off!

I have stated it was a slow time. I did not mind, considering it gave me a swell chance to adjust to my super new wings. I'd not quite got the hang of untethered free flight as yet and kept crabbing to port. However, soaring, buzzing the Gate and listening to Heavenly choir music was most exhilarating. There wasn't a synthesizer to be heard. After my third go-round a large skein of hurrying angels, late for the meeting, whipped me into a touch of wind shear and I crash landed, with my back to the gate. Turning around, preparing once again to take up my duties, who should I see but IRS, reaching out to ring the entrance bell. Well, you could have knocked me over with a feather! I was so startled I accidentally blurted, "What in hell are you doing here?"

Never was chosen such a misdirection of words. I purely figured I was in for a lightning bolt any second. Surprisingly, except for a winglike clacking and one peal of thunder, nothing untoward happened. You can make book, Heaven — for certain — had already heard of IRS. She cooed about how her life was dull without me. Nobody complained. It was too quiet. She especially missed the quaint endearments I employed, and how red my face got when I hollered them in her ear. "Nay" she wailed, "I miss you too much to live apart. I am here, dearest, so that once more we shall live and love as one, enjoined and inseparable."

Lemme draw you a picture of IRS. First, she had what is called an hourglass figure. Time is money, right? Being a tad top-heavy, visualize her wound down and stopped at half-past two. Eyes, constantly blinking like a cash register, were dollar signs. Mouth, wide as an ancient alligator, playfully snapped shut every thirty seconds. Skin, dingy and curling, was a sand-blasted green color. Her legs were pipe stems, except for knobby knees where the taxpayers' loose change had congregated. A flaming Olive Oyl — there may be satisfaction in gorging on greenbacks, but there's no protein in them — she portrayed a frazzled, wrinkled, stale potato chip!

Got the picture? Can you imagine being stuck with her ... FOREVER?

This required sorting out. I knew her flipping credentials would read perfect. For crying in the flaming beer, her whole life was checking and double checking the accuracy of forms! Dismally, with no help for it, I had to follow Saint Peter's orders.

"Okay, IRS, but first you gotta spell a word."

"Sure," says the smug old bat. "What's the word?"

"Take a shot at, SUPERCALIFRAGILISTICEXPIALIDO-CIOUS!"

THE
PEARLY
GATES

Don't tell me that once in a while a dream doesn't come all dickied out in a lovely silver lining.

➳➳➳ ⬳⬳⬳

Although no longer housing animals, excepting for Miss Meg and a bevy of cats, Mojac Farm remained our home, but what do you do with an energetic Border collie who no longer runs sheep? Megan was family, no way were we going to become separated. Luckily, Mollie-O's brother, Dave, deciding to bunk with us, solved the problem.

Serving in the Marines in the South Pacific during World War II, he fought in the battles for Guadalcanal, Tarawa, Saipan and Tinian. He received battlefield promotions, eventually rising to the rank of major. He was also awarded the Bronze Star. Upon cessation of hostilities he served in China for another year, at Chinwangtao, protecting the railroad to Tientsin from the communists. (China has since changed those two names to, Qinhuangdao and Tianjin — I think!) Fair skinned Dave, while strolling around quaint little islands in the Pacific without his hat, had crisped his dome!

Through the following years, as Mollie-O's bro trudged the byways of life in California, his skin decided to get even for that early crisping and rewarded him with small — but potentially dangerous — cancers. As he aged, the little beauties hatched more frequently, requiring surgery. He began to order sun screen tubes by the gross.

Convinced a damper climate might help, and having heard the rumor that occasionally the giant spitter in the sky goes for broke and buckets down in good old Webfoot Land, Davey moved north to Mojac's, Wring Out Lodgings. Newly retired from the Los Angeles Police Department, having served for thirty plus years, he offered to baby sit Megan while we were off schooling. Once again our favorite Marine charged to the rescue, semper fidelis.

Partners in mischief, in a jiffy the pair became inseparable. If I needed Dave, I'd look for Meg, need Meg, look for Dave. It got so bad, I stopped asking the Marine for the events of his day, I questioned Megan! Davey also introduced Meg to her third great joy —

FRISBEE! He dad-blamed well gets the rap for bringing on her third irritating habit, too — DROOLING.

Dave is a large man, very conversant with food; in fact, anytime a lull interrupted gabbing with neighbors, he and Megan would raid the frig. There resided on the outskirts of town a drive-in hamburger joint. Later, known far and wide as the Dave and Meg Grit Palace. Those two would always stop there for a snack (between meals) when heading in to the big city to shop for food to restock the now empty frig! Besides sheep, the second word memorized correctly in Megan's vocabulary read, chow. Comfy in the back of Dave's wagon, she'd watch one double with extra cheese slide down the gullet of the malnourished Marine. Correction, that's not quite accurate, only about half disappeared, ere Meg pushed her nose in and got the other half. Davey would order another, and the desperate fight to ward off malnutrition then repeated.

Before long, whenever Cooky observed those two scoffers cruising in, he automatically threw an extra on the grill for Megan: hold lettuce, pickle, mayo, and catsup. Forever after, upon Mojac's returning to their wagon, the awaiting Megan, looking for handouts, would slobber. Gee, thanks, big brudda!

Frisbee became Megan's salvation and her absolute passion. Yet, in the beginning, she wouldn't, or couldn't, catch diddly. Dave was unskilled at throwing the flaming thing and Megan hadn't the foggiest idea what she was supposed to do. Once in awhile Herself might deign to retrieve that plastic nothing and drag it back to the guy who'd fluffed it, but as it wasn't a bone, boredom soon set in and she went back to chasing birds!

Snow quilted the pastures when the airborne answer, for Megan accidentally whizzed by an inattentive ear; 'twas the day of the miracle!

Dizzy Dean Dave uncorked a real hummer. That spinning platter cruised by Megan's ear just as her head turned. Surprised, it was either catch the sucker or wear it! Jerry (Megan) Rice snagged that whizzer in her jaws and her second life began to etch into history, folks. Mojac Farm became frisbee heaven for her. Davey taught her that old 'statue of liberty' football play, which could be somewhat hazardous to his loose fingers. He even trained Megan to

MEG
AND
FRISBEE

stay onside before his called out signals would release her for a Marine — hand grenade special — long bomb! They practiced by the hour; NFL scouts began to take notice.

Miss Jaws would utterly destroy a disc in a single day because she was always downright determined to hang on and the cheap plastic could not defy her canine crunchers. We finally blew the alfalfa dust out of Mojac's purse and bought a proper pet frisbee, made of neoprene. For the rest of her days Meg teethed on that zoomer without managing to annihilate the dear thing.

Our Frisbee Champ was also quite vain, in fact, she became an out and out egotist! Later in Meg's life, after Mollie-O and I'd joined the Geritol Set in retirement and Davey had returned to California, I was shanghaied into becoming thrower numero uno. She wouldn't get off my back unless I plucked the gummy old thing off my shoes (where she had conveniently dropped it) and followed her dancing feet outdoors. I discovered her vanity on a day when, with her closed jaws still firmly gripping the prize after a lunging catch of a fifty yarder, she barked! A loud, explosive bark of satisfaction that proclaimed her amazing feat to all onlookers. I had never known that a dog could bark with its muzzle closed. Confounding further, Megan only voiced that swagger bark after a great catch.

Megan was also a divil of a bit sly. Playing football with her, if she thought I wasn't looking, she would sneak offside. I always nailed her. "Bad dog, there are rules to this game. That just cost you a big five yards!" She would lay her canine grin on me, roguishly roll

MEG AND FRISBEE

those expressive brown eyes, accept the penalty, and then blink back at me, "Go ahead and stiff me ump. I'm the west wind and I'll catch that flyin' scudder even if you tack on an extra fifteen!" Megan never failed to make good her brag. She absolutely adored frisbee. Under any and all circumstances: rain, snow, sleet, aching old bones or dinner time, she would drop everything to snatch an aired spinning disc that dared to try escaping. Once those jaws closed tight, here came the exultant bark. Filled with herself — plume waving — she would then prance proudly back, ready to race for one more record setter. Her conceit was downright nause-ating, but, oh, how I wish I could throw her that one more.

I should also add that thanks to that frisbee exercise, not to mention the ten minute jobs, Dave's health, smog free, had greatly improved. In fact, considering all those between lunch and dinner hamburgers, without it they would both have been as fat as ... Gutface!

-》》 《《-

Readers all, please do not run out and purchase a Border collie without your full acceptance of the fact that they are active, energetic, thinking dogs who demand work. Ignore at your peril. If you remember, the huggable but bored Border collie — like the tax collector who has to give some back — does not get mad, they get even! To purchase one, simply because they are smart, loyal, attrac-tive and cuddly, would not be fair and benefit neither you — nor the dog.

16

Meg: The Funny and the Hard Part

Other than imprinted behind our eyes, would that a
rainbow last.

Mojac

Farewell to pretty Mojac Farm. We missed our animals. I would miss Cuthbert, and Chesley. I'd even miss Cecil, Bertram, Chauncey and Chumley, although, lest we get carried away here, not enough to desire renewing acquaintance. I would truly mourn ancient Alfred, that curmudgeonly old tractor — that scheming machinator whose one goal was to break down every time the job that couldn't wait, wouldn't wait! We'd miss our frogs, Meg's pond, the barn, the beauty, and the quiet.

In order to live and flourish, a farm must be worked. Social Security is nice, but it won't lay out the kind of dinero needed to buy hay for livestock, nor will it come across with the financing Mojac would require in order to purchase a new tractor and allow Alfred to retire. In truth, if escalating Medicare premiums and supplemental insurance costs, right along with "figure out a way to raise 'em" taxes, don't simmer down, it's not even going to cover the cost of a Big Mac!

Ten and one-half years of Mojac farming life, an eventful one hundred and thirteen months, ninety six of them enjoying the company of animal friends, had swooshed on by. Someday — when and if I'm combing angel feathers — the gang will all be there: E. Flynn, Sir Francis, Filet and Mignon, Sheba, Squeaky, Bandita, Packy and Derm, Peppy and Buttercup. Surrounded by all our pals, Mollie-O and I will be holding hands. Megan, her head resting upon my knee, her grungy frisbee mucking up my feet, will be eye-begging me to toss the longest of long ones. Sheep sheared, wool sacked, nary one forkful of phewey-phewey left in the barn; the Farmall not only running, but purring; sun shining, clouds smiling, and our frogs harmonizing in a special Mojac operetta, while lambs gambol on lush green pastures or ... I'm not staying!

➤➤➤   ⫷⫷⫷

Ready for sad tidings? A few years after we sold the farm, a vile calamity, irremediably severe, struck our precious barn. The bonehead to whom we sold the place, accidentally but carelessly, burned it down! Mojac's animal haven — our gracious welcoming old love — has been reduced to an ugly pile of dirty black cinders. I can't talk about it anymore.

➤➤➤   ⫷⫷⫷

Free of the farm, living was still rich for Megan, Mollie-O and me, including a jaunt to San Diego for a visit with Dave. Miss Megan motored along with us for two reasons: fat chance of slipping away without her, and Dave's hospitable invitation, which read, "Come and enjoy the sun for as long as desired, just make sure you bring Megan, too!"

What with travels, frisbee and more time at the beach, Megan, happy and contented, was dining off the meaty ribs of life. Most of the time, Herself remained a good neighbor. When in her Buick station wagon, she would mouth off to passing cousins, kissing or otherwise, but those exchanges noised mostly political, airy and meaningless. Parading her Border good nature in community living, Megan wagged friendly to dog and cat alike, until ... a certain Doberman! Two blocks west and one block south there dwelt — Siegfried. His owners were in the habit of walking their four pets, he being one, past Meg's domain on a regular basis. In loud canine disputation, insults were exchanged. Three of the dogs ignored the Mojac Mouth, but not Herr Siegfried. It happens that way. There are those, including Mojac's Megan, who take bad talk most seriously; therefore, she developed an intense unneighborly dislike for the Dobie.

One day, while Mojac busied themselves on yard work, the exercise gang strolled by. Meg, prone on the floor in the garage door entrance was on a "stay" but not on leash. Siggy hurled something unforgivable at her, and Megan had had enough. She just had to have a piece of that boy! Outweighing her by twenty-five pounds, he also loomed a foot over her in height. Regardless, my Megan came from a long line of those we call courageous. She was on him like a gift of claw from a wildcat. Fearfully, as our little piece of coast immediately turned into a snapping, snarling donnybrook, I threw my cringing bod smack into the middle of that outraged medley of mutt melee! Mediation is not my specialty. Consequently, probing here, snatching there, I finally snagged the Dobie and gently tossed him half a block away. Next, I grabbed Megan by the head and tail and sailed her into the garage, followed by an emphatic "STAY!"

Puffing and gulping for air, I surveyed the field of battle and counted heads. Herself was an obedient lass, and always followed orders except ... not this flaming time!

Meg's Scot's blood was up, and I'll be a soft breeze in a bad hurricane if that snarling collie dervish hadn't circled around behind me and headed right on back for another chunk of Siegfried! Would it amaze you to discover I was a shade out of patience by then? Collaring Rocky one more time, her feet hit the pavement but once before she was incarcerated behind closed doors in the house. From there, imprecations horrible in the extreme, were cast on the Doberman including all his ancestors.

Wheezing, I politely suggested another route might be best for the quartet when next taking their nature walkie-walkies; then I hobbled into the house for another rare, nose to nose, discussion with Her Majesty.

From that day forward, whenever Megan, on lead and walking, sighted Siegfried, also on leash and a long block away, she growled, her hackles rose and she crouched into her herding stalk. Waving to our neighbors, and extending "bon chance" greetings to the Doberman, we would signal intent to head north; responding, they hiked south or we'd vice versa. I took Megan's growl to read: "You've got a face like a wet week, turkey. Someday we'll duke it out again!" Some folks would rather eat the dove of peace!

➼➤   ⬅⬅

We have almost come full circle, and I guess my narration wouldn't be complete without including a further couple of incidents Mollie-O has been bugging me to relate, as to how we originally discovered a need for Megan. I apologize for being tardy with these insertions. I've only delayed, because they don't exactly portray me at my unruffled best.

"Quit blathering and get on with it."

"I've already told about Meg and her hidey-hole."

"No, no, no," she chortles. "I am referring to the real reasons."

"The real reasons make me look stupid!"

"I sympathize (she doesn't sympathize at all!), however, in the interests of accuracy, if what you have related is a true narrative, oblige your readers and present all the facts."

I can see I'll never enjoy one iota of peace until I do.

Reluctantly then, here is the true, unvarnished version of why the necessity for Megan arose. Reader friend, a touch of sympathy from you, would not go amiss:

Within a month of the farm's purchase I noticed one of our ewes, a mother with lamb, was limping and favoring her right front leg. Remember, city life was my bailiwick, what did I know of limping legged ewes? Early on at Mojac Farm, if in doubt, phone the vet. A telephone call to the Doc — a most laconic man — was an education in itself. Upon his answering, I would immediately launch into an explanation.

"Hello Sam, this is Jack at Mojac Farm, up in the hills. I have a limping ewe, can you come?"

Seemed like ten minutes passed, then Sam would inquire, "A limping sheep?"

"That's right, Sam, she is limping quite badly, can you come?"

After passage of another ten minutes, "Back leg or front?"

"Front, Sam."

Lengthy wait, "Left leg or right?"

"Right, Doc."

Long pause, "What seems to be wrong?"

"We don't know, Sam, that's why I've called, can you come?"

Silence lingers, "I guess I can come, what's the address?"

My phone conversations with Sam always went like that. He was never, ever in a verbal hurry. All the same, he was a kind and gentle man, no matter what the condition of road or weather, Doc would always come to your aid.

Mollie-O and I'd housed ewe and lamb in the barn while waiting for the vet; I lured her in with jelly beans. (It bears repeating, "city boy"!) When Sam ambled into the picture, after observing the wary duo, the big one hobbling, he drawled, "I guess you better catch the ewe and I'll look her over."

Full of shepherd lore and confident, figuring I could reach out and casually snag her, I moved in on the limper and did just that; at least, I attempted to do just that. Three legs or no, she easily evaded my clumsy grab and then, closely followed by her lamb, gazelled to the other end of the barn. Undaunted, I reached for her again. Zoom, the two jetted back to their original launching pad. I have to tell you my friends — catching that ewe was like trying to slip socks on an octopus!

Undefeated, I headed for her once more. Hemming them closer into a corner I decided to fake momma out; they hadn't named me, Wee Woollie, linebacker of the year, for nothing. Calling out signals, I leaned right and dived left. The flaming gazelle gave me a hip and, eeling by, performed a perfect Marcus

Allen, three legged ewe, toe-dance down the sideline for a long touchdown.

Unable to stop my dive, I plunged face down in a pile of phewey-phewey! Sam nearly shattered his jaw trying not to laugh. Not so Miss Mollie. Surfacing, spitting, my ears detected half-stifled feminine snickers. I had also forgotten the lamb. Surprised by ma's move he'd remained behind, but not for long. Uttering a loud baa-a, junior high-jumped — landed squarely in the middle of my back, dunked my schnoz deep in that muck one more time — and three seconds later he had rejoined mom. As I emerged, spraying once again, I was entertained by the wholehearted, tear-trickling, knee-slapping, har-har-hars airing from the female set, (including the ha-ha-ha, crippled ewe)!

You're flaming right, there truly are days when one genuine, Ralph Kramden, moon shot is a warm, comforting, thought.

By and by, my vision and breathing restored, their convulsing suspended, El Medico quietly suggested I use a portable gate in order to corral our swivel-hipped ewe; this I promptly did. (It was here I learned the true value of this already mentioned handy tool.) Piece of cake after that. I begged honor to shoot the ewe, medicinally of course. Hoof soaked and salved, mother and lamb contentedly munching after all that exercise, put an end to Sam's first visit to Mojac Farm; it would not be the last. We began to search for Megan the next day. Reminiscence is not always accurate, but this I know, for many months after — on windy days — whenever I entered the barn, I swear that creaking rafters nudging the roof sounded exactly like rude laughter. Insensitive sods!

There was one other incident prior to the limping ewe which also led us in the direction of a Megan, and it happened the morning after the day Mollie-O and I began our life on Mojac Farm. The month was early April, 1977.

Having bought the little beauty, we moved in, eagerly antici-pating our first wonderful, lung-filling, clean-air day in the country. School was still in session. Accordingly, rising early I fed the stock, then happily readied my quaking bones to ask Blackie to lead the sheep to the pasture I had chosen for them to enjoy for the day. Among the reams of sage advice I had tried to absorb from the previous owner, I remembered the importance of rotating hungry sheep from pasture to pasture to prevent overgrazing.

"Just call for Blackie," he had advised. "She will tootle forth from the barn to where you stand quivering. The rest of the girls will trot out after her. You will then stride manfully and confidently toward your field of choice, Blackie and the rest of her broads will follow. In a trice, your whole flaming flock will be grazing on fresh grass. Piece of cake."

Swinging the paddock gate open I called, somewhat timidly, "Blackie? If it is not too much trouble would you be so kind as to bring yourself and the other ladies out now?"

Well, I'll be a field of poppies smilin' in the sun, if Blackie and crew didn't perform exactly as touted. Daintily, demurely, the flock trotted after the old girl while she trotted after me. I casually ambled through the chosen pasture gate, wished each a pleasant day, locked them in, ho-hummed, and like a veteran shepherd, strolled calmly up to the house. I even had time for another cup of heavenly coffee!

Next morning, I literally leaped out of the sack — a modern miracle in itself — tripped gaily down to the barn to feed our dear sheep, wished all the girls a jolly good morning, dispensed hay and grain and then I summoned the parade forth again.

"Blackie dear. Please to follow me. The birds, in yon chosen field, are singing sweet songs in your honor."

Sweet and faithful Blackie, she led the flock forth, so friendly and eager. Rapport had been established, it was plain, ewe and I were of one mind.

Another gorgeous morning, I breathed deeply and stepped out toward the day's field. It was a beautiful start until, Blackie hung an unscheduled left turn.

"No, no, dear one," I called. "You're spending the day over in *this* pasture, not that one."

Madam B, by now nearly ninety degrees east of me, chose that moment to shift rapidly into second gear.

"Whoa, you silly thing," I hollered. "You're heading the wrong way," I quickly headed over to cut her off, but the old bag, thundering now, shifted into high and led her cronies due east toward an open-gated, already closely cropped pasture. Sprinting in pursuit, desperate to thwart her, my flying feet tripped over a half submerged rock causing me to ground loop on my nose! Adding insult to a bad landing, another of the sods, lurking by its side — tore a large hole in my arm. Somehow, it seemed like yesterday's harmony in song had become today's discordant babble.

Lying impaled on pointed granite I caught a glimpse of the last gleeful truant high-kicking into the forbidden pasture. Hoping I hadn't chipped a tooth, I pried myself off the mother of all boulders, limped over and eye-balled the disobedient one.

"Blackie, me old dear, could it be we differ over grazing rights? Why didn't you tell me the choice for the day was totally unacceptable? I'm sure we could have worked something out. Tell you what, let's call today 'ladies stroll where they wish day'. It's getting late, my arm is definitely in need of stitching and I also must away to school. Perchance we shall all renew friendly acquaintance again this evening. Oh, and do have a nice day!"

After wobbling up to the house for outpatient care, I casually informed Mollie, while iodine, clamps and bandage stopped blood flow, Mojac might be in need of a sheep dog. I bear the scar of that droll little episode to this day.

Little did we realize that the solution to our flock management problem would bring us so many years of joy and happy memories as well.

MEG AND
FRISBEE

I must relate another anecdote about our vet which occurred around eight years later: About the same time that Bandita was in the family way, my mother was looking for a kitten to maintain her greenhouse as a mouse-free zone. In due time, all was accomplished and Bandita presented Mojac with a litter of little bandits. Desiring a female, once the kittens were old enough to leave their mother, Mom chose one and named her Muffy.

Not wanting to fill the county with unwanted future generations, when Muff's age for spaying arrived, Mollie-O and I were asked to transport my mother's pride and joy to the pet hospital for the operation. We delivered Muffy into Doc's tender care and arranged for an after school pickup. Sam was nothing if not practical and he would always schedule six or seven of these operations on the same day.

Accordingly, he anesthetized his seven patients. Then, scalpel in hand, he worked his way down the line.

Slice, remove, sew ... lovely.

Slice, remove, sew ... oh, that one was grand.

Slice ... what? ... bummer!

Muffy was not a female! A surprised Sam had merely assumed, based on Mojac's information, and he hadn't taken a closer look before prepping poor Muff for surgery. He stitched the cold-cocked cat back together, phoned and explained the goof. Both of us thought it a rib-tickler, but the blunder left my mother furious. In his laconic drawl, Doc advised us to wait a few more months before we again tried to change the cat's — meow!

Funny, how thinking about a mangy, no-account dog brought all those farm incidents back so clearly in front of aging, near-sighted eyes.

⇉ ⇇

I caught her before she fell off the tailgate, set her inside, and only then realized I had just seen old age walk across the bed of the pickup. At that time Mojac was tootling around, for the most part, in a 1987, four-wheel drive Toyota, especially during our rare inclement weather. The pickup came equipped with a Gem top that sported two side windows and one facing the cab. They would all slide open as well as the one on the back of the truck cab. I built a portable bed, covered it with a soft but serviceable rug, and placed it in front of those two rear windows for the convenience of Her Majesty.

On warm days, we would slide both windows open and, perched upon her throne, Megan would thrust her head and shoulders into the cab in order to remind me to quit running the amber caution lights at intersections. Additionally, if we'd left anything valuable in the truck, besides Herself, she could be in front or back compartments in a flash. No one ever tried to find out if she was bluffing!

The tailgate lowered to about thirty inches off the ground. From a standing start, Megan would easily make the leap, then she'd nonchalantly strut back, ensconce herself upon her bed and smirk. Life, not a challenge for her, was good.

Came the day she missed her first leap. Forepaws scrabbling desperately and hind end hanging over the gate, she tried to hoist herself up. I was standing right there and quickly gave her a friendly boost into the back of the truck. We are all prone to miss our leaps from time to time, I said to myself, and thinking nothing of it, I closed pickup and Gem top backs and Mojac got underway.

Not long after, she failed to make the jump again. This time I caught a look almost of shame in her eye. She felt embarrassed, maybe even demeaned. For the first time, no longer taking her mortality for granted, I took a good long look at her. To my surprise, Meg's muzzle was graying and the brightness in her eyes seemed not quite as clear nor as confident; overnight, our Megan was picturing tired. She was growing old.

I hustled quickly to Sears and bought a two-step, molded plastic step stool, which included a top platform; that did the trick. Megan had always been a quick study and soon, via her stool, she was ascending and descending to and from her truck with ease. Her success did not last long enough to suit me. On a sad day, her bones too stiff to make the climb anymore, Meg stopped at the stool's base and, with the wise look of reality in her eyes, waited for me to pick her up and place her on the truck's bed. Displaying the grace and dignity so dominant in an adult Border collie, our dear one, resigned to her trouble, walked slowly to the welcoming bed and, with a small groan, laid her tired body down.

Mojac's Megan had, perhaps not willingly but certainly courageously, joined the advanced Geritol Set.

=>> <<=

Throughout Megan's final year, she was not her usual spry self. Frisbee still headed the list of her priorities, although catch had reduced mostly to chase. Food did not really hold interest. In fact, Meg had become downright obnoxious about dinner. Her diet had been modified to reduce protein and to protect her liver and kidneys. Consequently, according to Meg's tastes, we had her on a blah diet; healthy, yes, lip smacking good, no. She vented displeasure by noisily nose-pushing her dish of "stuff these grits" all over the floor! Journey's end became a kitchen corner where her entree plate ended up rudely stuffed under her security blanket — out of sight, out of mind. Then, positioned on her pillow, one baleful eye peeled for our reaction, Herself would wait.

Shortly, Mollie-O or yours truly would go and uncover the buried. Act two, promptly repeated, performed to the exact degree of act one until finally, whether from exercise or hunger, Megan la Grump deigned to dine. A final dab with serviette, her pillow doubling as a face wiper, and Megan, getting even, gave out with her imperious, demanding attention bark. Naturally, this resulted in Ma or Pa promenading the back acreage with Her Majesty, until she was good and ready to head back and hit the sack. Fortunately, diet and medicine both working, Megan thrived so well she was almost back to her old — clear the decks for action — pushy self.

Ultimately for us all the end of day means day's end. Not quite a full year later, Megan arrived at hers. Medicines, care, hope and love can only do so much; time runs out. When dearest Megan laid her tired old head down in a last and final sleep, she broke our hearts.

Mojac's Megan, our Border collie who was, will never be again. Mollie-O and I miss her terribly. And yet, closing my eyes on days when the missing becomes heavy, enjoying some private inward viewing I can still see Dave's air-waving legs, a laughing

Meg and a puzzled Gutface. I chuckle as I spy Meg's up close and personal "howdy" to the car thief. One quick blink of my eyes and there is Megan again, running rings around the panting, exhausted beach bum, or launching herself jubilantly into her pond for the umpteenth time. So clearly, I see Ol' Snake Hips dodging numerous lethal kicks from Willy and his gang — knowing any second she'll be turned into an arfburger — exhaling thankfully when it doesn't happen. I smile as Megan, the world's greatest frisbee catcher, is flagged for sneaking offside. So many scenes projected on the big screen of my mind. They always culminate with a small head coming to rest gently on my knee, and Megan's questioning brown eyes probing deeply, eloquently into mine.

How often soft rain, turning to showers, forms a rainbow. Conceived under one, Mojac's Megan remained our pot of gold for sixteen rewarding years. An order to report for duty has taken her from us. Away off in celestial places, I believe there are sheep — lost and lonely — that our Megan will find and bring safely home.

Megan of Mojac died March 12th, 1994. She rests among her friends where happy birds sing. A rose — Fragrant Memory — perfumes the air above her head.

Oregon's state motto captures the essence of Megan's life. "Alis volat propriis." She flies with her own wings. Today, dear Meg, it honors you.

Goodnight Sweet Megan: Full giving of your love — in honest return — you, too, were deeply loved. Sleep warm. Sleep well.

HEAVEN
BOUND

Author's note: In 1997, Connie Shoemaker, the artist at Summer Gap here in Lincoln City, Oregon, created and assembled a stained glass window. That window depicts two young children enjoying the ocean view from the shore. You can tell they are eager to challenge the waves. Beside them, in her protective pose, stands our Megan. Above, behold the youngsters' guardian angel. This delightful work of art has since been installed in the new edition to St. Augustine's Catholic church. It is clearly visible from Highway 101. If you're in the vicinity, stop by and say, "Hi". We know she'd love to meet you.

And so, the promise of a rainbow is fulfilled, Mojac's Megan does indeed, shine in the light.

HERSELF

Biography:

Jack Judge, a native of Canada, has been an Oregonian for thirty-five years. A Staff-sergeant in the Air Force during the Korean War, he was attached to the 10th Air Rescue in Alaska. Upon discharge he raised pet birds. Adventure called him to the jungles of South America for more exotic birds and animals. He met Mollie-O, his wife, while working for a Chevrolet agency in Redlands, California. She introduced him to the joys of teaching. Subsequently, they taught school in Salem for twenty-three years. When not flying, he spends time on travel and photography.

To order additional copies of

Mojac's Megan

Book: $14.95   Shipping/Handling: $3.50

Contact: **BookPartners, Inc.**
P.O. Box 922
Wilsonville, OR 97070

E-mail: bpbooks@teleport.com
Fax: 503-682-8684
Phone: 503-682-9821
Order: 1-800-895-7323